# CORPORATE CREATIVITY

# CORPORATE CREATIVITY
## Robust Companies and the Entrepreneurial Spirit

### Edited by Raymond W. Smilor and Robert Lawrence Kuhn

PRAEGER SPECIAL STUDIES • PRAEGER SCIENTIFIC

New York • Philadelphia • Eastbourne, UK
Toronto • Hong Kong • Tokyo • Sydney

**Library of Congress Cataloging in Publication Data**

Main Entry Under Title:

Corporate Creativity

Based on papers presented at a conference sponsored
by the RGK Foundation and the Institute for Constructive
Capitalism at the University of Texas in April 1983.
Includes bibliographies and index.
1. Entrepreneur—Congresses. 2. Business enterprises
—United States—Congresses. 3. Industrial management—
United States—Congresses. 4. Venture capital—United
States—Congresses. 5. Industrial promotion—United
States—Congresses. I. Smilor, Raymond W. II. Kuhn,
Robert Lawrence. III. RGK Foundation. IV. University
of Texas at Austin. Institute for Constructive
Capitalism.
HB615.B716  1984        338'.04'0973        83-24525
ISBN 0-03-070679-3 (alk. paper)

Published in 1984 by Praeger Publishers
CBS Educational and Professional Publishing
a Division of CBS Inc.
521 Fifth Avenue, New York, NY  10175  USA

© 1984 by Praeger Publishers

456789  052  98765432

Printed in the United States of America
on acid-free paper

# Preface

There has been concern recently that the United States is losing its technological edge, that we are falling behind, that we cannot keep up with competition, and that recession and unemployment are draining our economic vitality. A different point of view emerged from the conference on which this volume is based — Robust Companies and the Entrepreneurial Spirit, which was sponsored by the Austin-based RGK Foundation and the Institute for Constructive Capitalism at the University of Texas at Austin in April 1983.

The sense of the participants was that the United States is poised for a great surge in technological and business development, a step-function transformation triggered by our ability to commercialize original scientific advancement and to generate novel corporate structures. A fertile climate, we are told, now exists for the growth of both small and large companies, for entrepreneurs of all kinds, and for a whole new wave of creative and innovative managers. We can expect, our experts promised, virtually another social and economic revolution.

Several forces are shaping this emerging revolution:

1. *The sheer abundance of natural resources.* Historically, the United States had it all — petroleum, coal, forests, minerals — and in essentially unlimited quantities. Despite a variety of shortages, we still possess abundant natural resources. Perhaps our only real shortage in recent years has been one of imagination.
2. *Recognition of our international market.* The United States is engaged in a global economy. Dynamic companies are now operating in a much broader and far more competitive marketplace than in the past.
3. *The role of invention.* The discovery and development of new technologies, processes, and methodologies is inextricably tied to the ingenuity of the American character — to what Alexis de Tocqueville called, in his remarkable book *Democracy in America*, the greatest American trait, the willingness to innovate.
4. *Capital.* You need money to make money. A growing pool of capital is being created in the United States — from foreign

investment, from pension funds, from personal and corporate profits, from venture capitalists. Capital is the catalyst in the entrepreneurial chain reaction.

5. *The role of government as stimulator.* Increasingly, government is finding ways to encourage entrepreneurial activity through mechanisms ranging from investment incentives and tax reduction to grants for research and development.

6. Most important, *the entrepreneur.* People with raw energy and a proclivity for risk taking built this country. They are continuing to build it today, in new ways, with fresh ideas, breaking tradition — this willingness to take risks, as we see it, is our greatest tradition.

But society also owes something to business and to the entrepreneur: political stability, some agreed-upon rules of the economic game, a relatively reliable monetary system, and the freedom to innovate.

The dynamic and intense entrepreneurial process relies on a simple formula: release talented people in an environment that respects the human quality to strive, to persevere, to surmount, and to achieve.

# Acknowledgments

This book is the result of the entrepreneurial spirit of several people and organizations.

Dr. George Kozmetsky, director of the Institute for Constructive Capitalism and chairman of the RGK Foundation, epitomizes the finest qualities of the entrepreneur in both business and academia. His commitment to entrepreneurial education and his dedication to linking theory with practice are the driving forces behind the conference and this book.

Ronya Kozmetsky, president of the RGK Foundation, provided invaluable direction in preparing and running the conference. Her administrative expertise and logistical savvy are indispensable; her untiring energy is almost impossible to match; and her commitment to the educational process is inspiring.

The student coordinating committee that managed the conference continually demonstrated one of the fundamental characteristics of entrepreneurs: insane persistence in the face of overwhelming obstacles. They are David Vitanza (chairman), Peter Zandan, James Barshop, Randy Pullman, and Martin Phillips.

We wish to thank Marilyn Kistner and Margo Latimer of the Institute for Constructive Capitalism for their assistance in planning the conference. We are grateful to Cynthia Smith of the RGK Foundation for her organizational expertise.

Myrna Braziel of the RGK Foundation deserves special recognition. She transcribed the entire taped proceedings and typed all the revisions with grace, good humor, and phenomenal efficiency.

We are indebted to the RGK Foundation and the Institute for Constructive Capitalism. Their commitment to entrepreneurial education is reflected in their steadfast willingness to commit resources to a continuing series of research projects, symposia, conferences, and publications.

We want to express our appreciation to George Zimmer at Praeger for his interest and encouragement and to Patty Gordon Sullivan at Praeger for her invaluable help in preparing the manuscript for publication, and to Susan Badger at Praeger and Rebecca Schorin at the Institute for Constructive Capitalism for their copyediting assistance.

We are grateful to those academics and practitioners whose contributions make up this volume and to those who energized the conference as discussion leaders.

Finally, jointly authoring a manuscript is like working in an entrepreneurial joint venture. Both demand long hours of work, an eye for evaluating progress critically, and a sense of humor. While we appreciate the contributions and the critiques of everyone who has participated in this volume, each of us wants to emphasize that the other takes full responsibility for any errors.

# Contents

# Introduction

A robust company, in addition to possessing operating strength and vigor, is firm in its purpose and visionary in its outlook. *Robust* implies a rough-edged quality that is characteristic of organizations, whether new or mature, small or large, that are adaptive to new developments in the marketplace, that maintain strength by ever changing in response to environmental stimuli. Robust companies are wily and tough, displaying an ability to learn from mistakes and a willingness to take calculated risks. They are dynamic organizations continually demonstrating an entrepreneurial spirit.

The future of the United States depends on our collective capacity to create robust companies by encouraging entrepreneurial activity. Robust companies provide more new jobs, show greater productivity, take advantage of innovations more quickly, compete in world markets more successfully, and in general make better use of our nation's human intellectual and technological resources.

This volume is dedicated to enhancing our knowledge of robust companies and the entrepreneurial process. It ties practice to theory and theory to practice, building pragmatic benefit from general principles and developing general principles from real-world activities. The chapters juxtapose business experiences and insights with academic concepts and analysis. In this way they provide guidance to the aspiring entrepreneur, wisdom for the experienced businessman, and substrate for the serious scholar.

The volume is organized in four parts. Part I sets the parameters of the entrepreneurial process by providing an analytical overview and an assessment of the sources of capital for small businesses.

Part II focuses on the drivers for entrepreneurial activity: the characteristics of the individual entrepreneur; the internal organizational factors necessary for success in new ventures; the role of government in encouraging entrepreneurial activity; and regional factors that provide a fertile environment for entrepreneurial activity.

Part III considers *intra*preneurial activity — entrepreneurship in large companies. Executives from three major U.S. firms present chapters dealing with factors motivating entrepreneurial creativity in large companies; the identification and development of managerial skills, talents, and abilities required in larger, technically oriented firms; and key factors in the successful commercialization of science and technology.

Part IV deals with issues related to emerging companies: the importance of venture capital, the ability of small companies to compete with larger ones in the high tech industries, the social and economic requirements for the continued proliferation of robust high tech firms, and the characteristics of the management team in successful new ventures.

# CORPORATE CREATIVITY

# Part I

# Defining the Entrepreneurial Process

## Chapter 1

# The Entrepreneurial Elements: Fire in the Belly and Brains in the Head

## Robert Lawrence Kuhn

Human beings are strange creatures. Just scribble a person's name on a stock certificate, and he or she will work longer hours, endure more hardships, suffer more abuse, absorb more stress, and earn less money. Why? Is the inducement merely the prospect of making more money in the long run? That is part of the answer — but only part.

Most people would love to own their own business, to be their own boss. They imagine going to work in the morning without a superior to serve or a time clock to punch. A rugged individualist is the image, a person forging his or her own path, creating his or her own destiny. Of those who take the plunge, a few prosper, most fail, and all struggle. And yet the glamour remains: It is the great American dream.

More than dollars are involved. Personal achievement more than organizational security motivates the typical entrepreneur. The business must become the most important thing in the world. It must *be* the world, at least for a time. The sun must rise and set on the daily sales report, on the monthly P & L's (profits and losses), on the payroll taxes, and on cash flows. The entrepreneur must burn with his idea; he must be obsessed with its success and consumed by its passion. Wholehearted commitment, monastic dedication, intense energy, and great perseverance — these are the critical ingredients for success. Starting your own business has been compared to keeping an ever-demanding mistress content.

There are, however, no cookbook recipes for entrepreneurial triumph. Add everything conventional wisdom requires, and failure is often the outcome. Leave out the commitment, dedication, energy, or perseverance, and disaster is almost surely the result. When dealing with start-ups, it is far easier to predict failure than to prescribe success.

Going into business for yourself is a life-affecting decision. It will dominate your every working hour and absorb most of your other ones. Recent research on entrepreneurs reveals some interesting, perhaps startling, characteristics. In general, independent, successful businessmen are not necessarily the smartest (cerebral types are more interested in theory); not necessarily the best students (some had dropped out of school; some had even been expelled); not the most stable (they often came from uprooted and immigrant families); not the best employees (many had been fired from previous jobs); certainly not comfortable around subordinates (generally they only trust other entrepreneurs); and not viewers of spectator sports (they are active, not passive, types and prefer to participate). All in all, an entrepreneur is one rare bird.

Entrepreneurship is the driving energy of the new world of business, a world that encompasses a broad base of traditional organizations and innovative institutions — profit-making, quasi-profit-making, not-for-profit, governmental, and intellectual. Let us ask some questions. What are the social benefits of small business? How should small businesses be run? What are the critical success strategies? How do you make entrepreneurial decisions? What role can the business school play? And finally, a self-test: What is your E.Q.? That is, what is your "entrepreneurial quotient," or should you start your own business?

The widening impact of the field requires a broadening definition of the term. Business is the economic synthesis of human knowledge, the molding of physical substance and value out of mental form and concept. Business is the modern human analogue of the original Genesis creation when chaos and void were transformed into heavens and earth. Business is the process that produces something from nothing.

Business is also exciting — the hope of the big hit, the tension of uncertain outcome. What makes business exciting for the individual person is the energy that empowers collective society and drives human progress. Of the top 100 firms in the United States in 1918, less than half were even recognizable in 1968.

## THE SOCIAL BENEFITS OF SMALL BUSINESS

Creativity and innovation are our country's most valuable natural resources, easily accessible and readily renewable. And the key to stimulate creativity and fire innovation? Entrepreneurial motivation, the magnetic pull of proprietary ownership. As a matter of national public policy, mechanisms must be developed to maximize entrepreneurial motivation in order to optimize social and economic benefits. Incentive generation is vital because research and innovation are not the same thing. The former can be done on demand; the latter cannot. Research can be programmed from without; innovation must be generated from within. So we must accord inventors and innovators in all sectors of the economy – industry, university, government – full rights to their creations. Anything less will restrict the process and retard the economy.

In this context there is need for entrepreneurial education that encompasses the teaching of students as well as the instruction of practitioners. There is also need for long-term thinking among large company chief executive officers (CEOs). CEOs must be encouraged to see beyond their own tenures of office, even beyond their stock option plans.

It is a wondrous time for entrepreneurs. Science and technology have created remarkable business opportunities. To take but one example, just in the last few decades some 6 million new chemicals have been synthesized or discovered compared with less than 2 million in all prior recorded history. The exponential growth of biologically based businesses will be absolutely unprecedented. Where molecular biology was 20 years ago, genetic engineering is today. Where neuroscience is today, who knows what we will be doing with the brain in the year 2000.

Some caution is called for here. There are substantial skill distinctions and cultural differences between scientists and inventors, on the one hand, and businessmen and managers, on the other. Each group, of course, can produce its share of company successes. Indeed, some scientists make good businessmen, but this is not often true. Furthermore, entrepreneurial characteristics are not synonymous with either group, yet both scientists and managers may be entrepreneurs. *To start your own business you need fire in your belly as well as brains in your head.* Frankly, it is usually critical to couple a scientist/entrepreneur with seasoned businessmen, professionals experienced with running new enterprises, savvy street-smart managers who know the meaning of marketing, finance, credit, budgeting, accounting controls, manufacturing, distributional systems, customer relations, organizational structure, strategic management – the list is endless. But if we get so intoxicated by the scientific side that we neglect the business side, we will be sending both good money and good ideas down the same drain.

A radical shift is occurring in the fundamental structure of the economy. Traditional manufacturing, however revitalized, must give ground to other sectors. Even high technology, although surely a subset of manufacturing, has a different cast to it. Employees have a new mentality, and the management of technology has become an important area for organizational study and innovation.

Information-based businesses are perhaps the greatest growth area. Both the means of communication and the data bases themselves are novel elements not long in existence. Future managers must be trained to be fully facile with the issues and problems unique and germane to these unchartered regions.

The increasing importance of not-for-profit institutions – hospitals, schools, universities, museums, foundations, churches – requires area-specific managerial training, not just the assumed applicability of manufacturing-oriented business education. Future leaders of such institutions must be as sophisticated in first-rate management know-how as they are dedicated to their organization's laudatory goals.

Government as well must benefit from the expertise derived from the competitive demands of the private sector. The reality of continuing efforts to build bridges between government and industry creates two-way flows of benefits. It enables our public servants to learn management techniques and systems from private executives, and it allows government to better serve the interests of business through more efficient regulatory procedures.

Small business, some people say, is an endangered species. For years their percentage of national assets and profits has been eroded by the voracious growth of corporate giants, the industrial behemoths that gobble and expand like monsters from a 1950s science fiction movie. Learned economists and fierce lobbying groups line up on both sides of the political fence, arguing vigorously for their own self-serving positions. The progiant contingent extends Darwin's "survival of the fittest" claim that if small companies cannot hack it in the marketplace, they should be driven from the scene. If our huge, highly efficient businesses are artificially restrained from government regulation, they maintain, the United States will be pushed progressively out of world markets both by product and price, with ever-increasing balance of payment problems the inevitable result. Laissez-faire, "leave us alone," the big boys inform Washington, and whatever will be should be.

The small business lobby, on the other hand, has massive clout. They come to Washington with a long shopping list in one hand and a large ballot box in the other. They want tax benefits, less paper work, more contracts, special bidding, earmarked funds – not unreasonable demands. Small companies are a critical component of modern capitalism. They ensure the efficiency of the economic sector by restraining monopolies; at the same time, they secure the pluralism of the political sector by disrupting the hegemony between big business and big government.

But small businesses must not be kept alive by artificial means. For not unlike brain-damaged humans maintained by machines, they would become living vegetables, objects of dole and pity, relics of the past, wards of the state, drained of vigor and energy, slowly degenerating, losing resolve and life force, devoid of worth or value. The only thing more tragic than the failure of small firms in the marketplace would be their counterfeit survival in the iron lung of bureaucracy.

Self-determined strategy is more precious than government-imposed regulation. The former is hard and sure; the latter is loaded with whim and caprice. Small companies must survive and prosper within the free market system, not outside of it. They must compete effectively and efficiently against the mammoths and the megaliths guarding and guaranteeing their own existence. Anything less is self-defeating for the firm and counterproductive for society. Life dependent on largess is life dependent on whim.

Perhaps the most widely repeated strategic axiom – and a mournful one indeed for small companies – concerns the relationship between profitability and market share. A difference of ten percentage points in market share has been shown to be accompanied by a corresponding difference of about five percentage points in pretax profits. On both sides of the production/marketing coin, big companies simply wield more power – economies of scale and procurement, manufacturing and other cost components, and greater market power in bargaining, pricing, and selling. The combination is potent; the results inevitable. For any given product, the dollars received go up and the cost per unit goes down; in the end large firms obtain higher profit – a simple success formula, to be sure, and a powerful pathway to oblivion for smaller firms.

Yet the hand may not be quite that pat, the script not that tight. For although the data may be accurate, the conclusions may not. In many industries, smaller companies outperform the larger ones: more profits and better performance – consistently. In fact, there are hundreds of medium-sized companies and thousands of smaller-sized companies that year in and year out achieve higher return on sales and equity than do their larger rivals. How do they do it? What are their critical success strategies?

## CRITICAL SUCCESS STRATEGIES

*Strategy* defines the relationship between an organization and its environment, integrating functional areas and driving the resource allocation process. Strategy is ideally generated by mapping the firm's strengths and weaknesses onto the market opportunities and threats in order to accomplish long-term goals and short-term objectives. *Creativity* is vital to strategy formulation just as *consistency* is to strategy evaluation and *structure* is to strategy implementation. Finding effective strategies is the search for competitive advantage, for areas of distinctive competencies where one firm has or can develop a competitive edge over the others.

Recent research has shown at least three areas in which small firms have such a distinct advantage: size, worker satisfaction and innovation. *X-inefficiency* is defined as the excess of unnecessary costs as a percentage of actual costs, and it increases with increasing size. What mechanisms are involved? Among them are executive softness nurtured by large profit margins, bureaucratic structure of large organizations, and the sluggishness of pure size. Thus the smaller firm can be inherently more efficient, and this is the beginning of comparative advantage.

There are other *dis*economies of pure size. Worker satisfaction – as determined by the nature of the work and social relationships within the firm – is reduced by the size of the company. Employees in bigger companies have higher degrees of personal alienation and lower levels of job contentment. Other things being equal, workers in smaller companies will produce more and be happier doing it. This, too, is comparative advantage.

Furthermore, small firms have comparative advantages in innovation. Innovation might be more compromised than enhanced in an economic environment populated only by giants. Research has shown that introduction of novel ideas takes place most often in medium-sized firms, those with roughly a 5 percent to 20 percent share of the market. It is common knowledge that revolutionary ideas germinate with highest frequency in small firms, companies with neither mental constraint nor prior predilection. This again spells competitive advantage.

My study of more than 200 top-performing medium-sized manufacturing companies has shown that firms need not be industry leaders to be successful. Indeed, one of my criteria of selection was that each of my top-performing medium-sized companies had to be in an industry dominated by one or more monster companies many times its size. Yet my smaller firms consistently outperformed their mammoth rivals. How did they do it? The reasons are crucial.

More important than government regulations far beyond a firm's control are the following critical success strategies well within its control.

*Dominate Your Corporate Niche*: Segment the market mercilessly. Narrowcast your products so that the firm can achieve and sustain maximum share within a minimum market. Define products and markets tightly. Segment by specific product, price, customer, quality, brand, distribution, geography, service; segment by *something*, but segment. Seek control through perceived superiority. Be a big fish in a little pond. Remember, small can still dominate.

*Be Product Oriented*: Give the company's products primary importance. Stress product focus, essence, name, and reliability. See the product from the customer's viewpoint. Never make the products subservient — not even to executive desire, not even to financial comfort.

*Be Distinctive/Unique*: Make the firm overtly different from competitors'. Strive for some originality, something to set the company apart in the perception of customers. Impact the end user.

*Strive For Focus/Coherence*: Establish goals, objectives, and strategies with clarity of thought and coherence of content. Build new businesses on the central core skills, resources, facilities, or managerial competencies of old businesses.

√ *Have a Committed, High-Profile Chief Executive*: The boss should generate personal charisma, a profound sense of dedication, an aura of excitement. He should generate intense levels of energy and have a desire, even a compulsion, to get involved all pervasively in every aspect of the business.

√ *Give Executives/Employees Opportunity*: Exploit the comparative advantage of smaller firms to attract entrepreneurial kinds of people and offer all employees greater job satsifaction. Be people oriented.

√ *Use Innovation/New Products Effectively*: Capitalize on the relative advantage of smaller firms to introduce new products sooner and more swiftly. Attack market leaders if they protect current market positions by withholding innovation (as they often do).

√ *Be Perceptive of the External Environment*: Stay attuned to market demands and customer needs. Have a keen sense of competitors. Be prepared for sudden discontinuities and be ready to exploit them. Turn on a dime.

√ *Evaluate the Growth/Profits Trade-Off Carefully*: Avoid growth for growth's sake, but seek growth for your business's sake. Market products forcefully. Visualize longer time horizons for profit return. The bottom line is all that counts, not the top one. Billion dollar corporations have gone bankrupt while very small companies have made their owners very rich.

√ *Be Flexible/Opportunistic*: Be ready to react to changes in markets or products. Retreat when the enemy attacks; attack when the enemy retreats.

Small businesses are what made this country great. Their survival and prosperity is a national necessity and a collective resource. But prosperity cannot be provided by external force. (Survival, maybe; prosperity, never.) Real success must come from internal sense, management savvy, and entrepreneurial guts.

A word of warning for the eager entrepreneur. The above-enumerated strategies are both obvious and simplistic; do not allow the former to discourage you nor the latter to fool you. The points are powerful, founded on data from hundreds of companies. Conversely, such simplistic advice must not be used as a magic wand, a panacea for confused entrepreneurs seeking direction — as all too often happens when management consultants spout their traditional wisdom. Generalized prescription, never forget, is one thing; realistic recommendation is quite another.

## MAKING ENTREPRENEURIAL DECISIONS

Let us go to decision making — what executives do often, what entrepreneurs do all the time. Decision making has essentially two modes, two approaches to the process: the incremental and the strategic. Operating in the incremental mode, the manager begins reactively by recognizing a problem, some unexpected shock, whether internal or external, large or small, opportunity or threat. He then searches heuristically through a restrictive variety of potential solutions, making marginal deviations from the status quo, analyzing each possibility in sequence. Deviations from current policies are widened progressively until the first satisfactory solution is found. It is accepted immediately, and all other alternatives, even if potentially better, are ignored. Herbert Simon and James G. March's "bounded rationality" is the keystone here. The executive can never know everything; so, if he wants to do anything, he must replace optimizing with "satisficing," the realization that problems need only be solved satisfactorily, not perfectly.

Operating in the strategic mode, the manager begins differently. He now moves *pro*active by first defining general goals and setting specific objectives. He scans the external economic environment, seeking opportunities and threats, and analyzes the internal company milieu, discerning strengths and weaknesses. He maps the latter onto the former and generates a comprehensive, even exhaustive, list of strategic alternatives. Each is assessed for probable consequences and internal consistency. Implementation, feedback, and control systems complete the process.

It is a common proclivity to judge incremental decision making, the first mode, as "bad," and strategic decision making, the second mode, as "good." But such simplemindedness is wrong. Each is good but in its own area. One would not resolve an urgent inventory crisis in the strategic mode just as one would not formulate a five-year plan in the incremental mode.

What about computers? Are they going to help us in making entrepreneurial strategic decisions? Of a certain kind, yes. For operational issues such as minimizing cost of ingredients, components, equipment, travel time, record keeping, and so on, computers are essential. For long-range planning, however, they are only a notebook. Computers are a powerful tool for data collection and analysis. But today's most critical need is not for more information but for less. We need data reduction techniques, not ones of accumulation. We need to strive for the directed synthesis of data, the intelligent search for meaning.

Computers are deterministic, brains probabilistic. It is impossible to program computers — however large the data base, however intelligent the software — to make truly strategic decisions. The dimensions are incompatible. Computers can crunch enormous numbers by brute force, but only brains can search selectively for order and innovation amid chaos and tradition. Quantitative techniques should lead to analytical rigor in decision making and not become a fancy excuse for its absence. Rational inquiry and nonrational insight should be complements, not opposites, in the search for solutions to complex modern problems.

Modern brain research has shown that one side of the cerebral hemisphere, usually the left, is logical and cognitive, while the other side, usually the right, is holistic and affective. The left brain dissects the pieces; the right brain synthesizes wholes. The left operates deductively and rigorously; the right, by patterns and images. Decision making involves the exquisite interweaving of programmable logic and analysis (the left brain) with nonprogrammable impression and insight (the right). An entrepreneur requires that both hemispheres be active. He must see both the forest and the trees.

Personal opinions and values used to be deemed irrelevant. Of course, they could never be denied. Now we take a different tack. We consider individual desire and intent perfectly respectable input for the decision maker. Intuition has come out of the closet.

We are coming to a new appreciation for the art of conceptualizing decisions while enhancing the science of analyzing them. A manager's subjective feeling should not be intimidated by objective tests, and executives should not be afraid to overrule and contradict the computer. But neither should they leap fearlessly to arbitrary conclusions. Wholly intuitive decisions can be dangerous. An executive should make nonrational decisions only when he has clearly understood the rational alternatives. Intuition and analysis must be tested against each other in a repetitive process, with each iteration bringing greater confidence.

Do motives count? They are vital to appreciate — conflicting ones all the more so. *Stakeholder analysis* is a qualitative methodology that segregates the relevant parties to a decision and projects the personal positions of each. What is everyone's motivation, his or her "stake" in the matter? Crucial here is an assessment of individual feelings and hidden agendas. Potential political standing and perceived career paths often are lurking just beneath the surface. Entrepreneurs, in general, are rather insensitive to such goings-on.

Are most executive decisions made rationally? If I say yes, that is not necessarily good; and if I say no, that is not necessarily bad. Decisions are made by people, and people are constrained by organizational traditions and manipulated by political bargaining. The inertia of functional departments to do things according to standard operating procedures is a potent regulating mechanism, just as the influence of powerful personalities is a reality of the corporate hierarchy. The pervasive strength and profound pressure of established bureaucracies — corporate staffs, assistants to, budget directors — is now recognized more as a focus of serious study than as the butt of ridiculing humor. *Networking* a company — discovering the channels in which decision-controlling influence flows — is often a shock to top management. How real power patterns are structured can differ markedly from the official organizational chart. Power in entrepreneurial firms flows directly from proximity, even *perceived* proximity, to the boss.

Is decision making different in different kinds of organizations? How to "cut and categorize" a company is vital to understanding it. Decision making is a function of the sociological structure of the ambient environment. Is the sector profit making or not-for-profit? Is the organization large or small? Is the product creative or repetitive? Is the level of management top or middle? Is the personality assertive or passive? Is the procedure individual or collective? For example, in a high technology company, how should the CEO direct the key research scientists? In a charitable foundation, what dollar value should be placed on subsidized concerts for poor children? In a manufacturing firm, what level of losses can be sustained before a division is dispatched? In the media, should a magazine publisher stop his editor from printing a story critical of a top advertiser?

While similar in superficial form, each decision differs in fundamental substance. The scientist is a creative sort perhaps not given to close supervision. The artistic enrichment of the kids defies quantification. The manufacturing division may become a vital resource in future years. The magazine may not exist at all without editorial freedom.

Entrepreneurial decisions, therefore, begin novel in character, vague in structure, open-ended in time horizon, uncertain in process, and ambiguous in content. Complex decisions in unfamiliar areas must be factored into simpler subdivisions and more familiar areas. Today, common routines and procedures are applied to a recurrent situation in a familiar process: problem recognition, diagnosis, solution search, alternative development, alternative analysis, preliminary screening, analytical evaluation, final choice, authorization, feedback, and review.

Are there different kinds of entrepreneurial decision makers? We can make some models and have some fun, as long as we do not take them too seriously. Let us consider two dimensions on our little two-by-two contingency table (see Table 1-1). As shown, "information required" and "dimensions of thinking" fill in our four

**Table 1-1**
Entrepreneurial Decision Makers

| | | Single | Multiple |
|---|---|---|---|
| **INFORMATION REQUIRED** | *High* | (high information, one dimension)<br><br>Computer program | (high information, many dimensions)<br><br>Alchemist |
| | *Low* | (low information, one dimension)<br><br>Dictator | (low information, many dimensions)<br><br>Scatterbrain |
| | | *Single* | *Multiple* |
| | | **DIMENSIONS OF THINKING** | |

*Source*: Compiled by the author.

boxes. If a decision maker uses low information and thinks in only one dimension, he is opinionated and independent; call him a *dictator*. If he uses high information but still thinks in only one dimension, he is analytical and rigorous; call him a *computer program*. If he uses low information and thinks in many dimensions, he is flexible and fleeting – a *scatterbrain*. If he uses high information and thinks in many dimensions, he is transformational and synthetic – an *alchemist*. Now the integrated attitudes of the last fellow would seem to make the most effective entrepreneur under normal circumstances. However, a company nearing bankruptcy might need a dictator; a mutual fund might want a computer program; and an advertising agency just might like a scatterbrain.

What is happening in our heads when we make decisions? Our brains cannot attend to more than one conscious thing at a time but can shift rapidly from one thing to another, like time-sharing in a computer. The neural apparatus called the *reticular activating system* highlights and habituates information, directing our attention. Furthermore, patterns of sensation can be traced throughout the brain, appearing not only in the higher conscious levels of the cerebral cortex but also in lower so-called subconscious areas. Between the two, data pass back and forth, being synthesized and transformed in the process. Waiting some time, therefore, to finalize crucial decisions could give these subtle systems a chance to work their magic.

For an entrepreneur, especially one whose company has enjoyed explosive administrative growth, "compromise" and "collaboration" are often in conflict. Compromise is a weak manager's failure to choose between contradictory positions or people. As such, the "in-between" solution can be worse than either of the extremes and no solution at all. To allocate to each of two competing projects half the money requested dooms both to certain disaster. Collaboration, on the other hand, brings the opposing parties onto the same side, encouraging iterative interplay, establishing the conditions for innovation. The dialectic of dissent, carefully controlled, is a marvelous antidote to the poison of groupthink. If collaboration is impossible, do not be coerced to compromise. Pick one of the alternatives and do not look back.

What is the critical test of a decision? I like to use internal consistency. Does the decision make common sense? Does it resonate with all relevant issues and areas? For example, is the decision to launch a new product consistent with all functional departments? Is production ready to make it, marketing ready to sell it, financing ready to pay for it?

Finally, what is recommended for the harried entrepreneur? Focus on the critical issue. Resolve the one and forget the others. What is the worst decision he can make? No decision — that is decision by default.

## THE ESSENCE OF BUSINESS EDUCATION

Business by its fundamental nature is categorically distinct from other academic areas, which are passive, pedagogical, and reflective rather than active, contributory, and interventional. History departments, for example, rarely affect current history; accounting departments, on the other hand, should affect current accounting.

The advancement of business knowledge is quite literally the growth of society. Business faculties occupy a unique position in the academic constellation. They have special opportunities to integrate and synthesize research from diverse areas. Work coming out of the physical, biological, and social science area is all germane to business investigation and becomes a substrate from which new concepts and creations are fashioned. Similarly, the potential interaction between university research and corporate research and development (R & D) offers critical-mass potential for new ideas, new ventures, and new systems. If economic development is dependent upon the birth of new knowledge, then the gestation should take place in business schools.

Graduate education in business is quite unlike graduate school in other disciplines; medicine, English, physics, and the like are cut from a different mold. In any of the normal content areas, knowledge and methodology are foundational to experience, and it would be nonsensical and contradictory to require prior work in the field as a prerequisite for study.

Business is different; it just is. Of course, a basic background is desirable, but frankly it is neither sufficient nor necessary for success. On the other hand, the educational process in business becomes exceedingly rich when it can play against the experiences of real life. Accounting problems leap out of the text; organizational development issues become important resources for salvation;

operations research techniques are viewed as new tools for problem resolution. An experienced manager hungers for further knowledge.

The scientific method is the core paradigm of modern man. Science itself is the foundation of many contemporary businesses. Business executives, consequently, must be literate in scientific methodology as well as content, and it is the duty of business schools to so educate them. Developing managers who can use computers as conceptual tools – for expanding horizons, for originality of thinking, and for moving and manipulating data and ideas – is a major task we now have.

Business schools must reach out, not back. No longer is the loop between academic business and corporate business a pattern of the former supplying the latter with fresh students and the latter supplying the former with fresh money. In our discontinuous economic environment, with ambiguity and uncertainty the rule and not the exception, with specialization and technology attaining new levels of sophistication, only a "new partnership" between the university and the corporation can ensure mutual prosperity.

Many large corporations today, recognizing the need to attract and retain business innovators, are devising unusual methods of autonomy and ownership. These methods are becoming accepted as a necessary part of modern corporate life – no matter how messy the intrusion on the classic organizational chart. (Have the Guts to Fail is the motto of one dynamic company.)

Entrepreneurship is now seen as a vital component of a healthy economy and forward-reaching companies. Courses are being offered by business schools and magazines cater to the start-up of new businesses. Entrepreneurship has become the national craze.

Although people decide to break into business at all ages – the stories of toddler tycoons and geriatric giants are not uncommon – the early thirties are the most likely age of decision. Many who go into business for themselves had fathers who did the same. Few entrepreneurs are ever ready to retire, and fewer still like giving up the reins without a fight.

## YOUR ENTREPRENEURIAL QUOTIENT

Still in the running? Let us test your E.Q., your entrepreneurial quotient, with these ten questions:

1. *Which do I prefer, job security or personal independence?*
   The entrepreneur is willing to risk bankruptcy in order to be his or her own boss.
2. *Is my business the most important thing in my life?*
   If it is not, you could be in big trouble striking out on your own.
3. *Am I willing to work 60 hours a week for poor wages for long periods of time?*
   You had better plan on working many more hours than that for a lot less pay, at least at the beginning. Work, for the entrepreneur, is its own reward.
4. *Can I take full responsibility for meeting my employees' payroll and paying my bills?*
   If you answer no, you should work for somebody else.
5. *Do I like to think about business at home?*
   You should if you are going into business, since that is exactly what you are going to be doing a lot of.
6. *Does my business idea have something unique about it, some unusual product to market, some special method to make it, some different place to sell it?*
   If not, you are going to be forever running uphill.
7. *Do I have to be told what to do?*
   If so, you need to be under a boss, not be one.
8. *How badly do I want to be my own boss?*
   The answer should be "plenty bad." You are going to have to put up with many irritating aggravations for little immediate reward.
9. *Which is more important to me, achievement or power?*
   A typical entrepreneur would rather market his or her own product from a garage than run a large corporate division from a six-window corner office.
10. *If given the chance to go into my own business, would I hesitate?*
    Most entrepreneurs would not hesitate a microsecond – but then again, most of them would fail in the enterprise.

Now, if you still want to go into business for yourself but have failed to meet any or even all of these criteria, take heart! Entrepreneurs, remember, do not make the mold; they break it!

# REFERENCES

Ansoff, H. Igor. *Business Strategy*. Harmondsworth, Middlesex, England: Penguin Books, 1969.

Bell, Daniel. *The Coming of Post-Industrial Society*. New York: Basic Books, 1973.

Brockhaus, Sr., R. H. "The Psychology of the Entrepreneur." In *Encyclopedia of Entrepreneurship*, edited by C. Kent, D. Sexton, and K. Vesper. Englewood Cliffs, N.J.: Prentice-Hall, 1982.

Carroll, P. J. "The Link between Performance and Strategy." *Journal of Business Strategy* 2 (Spring 1982): 3-20.

Chandler, A. D. *Strategy and Structure: Chapters in the History of American Industrial Enterprise*. Cambridge, Mass.: MIT Press, 1962.

Christensen, C. R., K. A. Andrews, and J. L. Bower. *Business Policy: Text and Cases*. 4th ed. Homewood, Ill.: Richard D. Irwin, 1978.

Cooper, A. C. "Entrepreneurial Environment." *Industrial Research*, September 1970.

Cyert, R. M., and J. March. *Behavioral Theory of the Firm*. Englewood Cliffs, N.J.: Prentice-Hall, 1963.

Drucker, Peter. *The Age of Discontinuity: Guidelines to Our Changing Society*. New York: Harper & Row, 1969.

Glueck, W., L. Jauch, and R. Osborne. "Success in Large Business Organizations: The Environment-Strategy Connection." *Academy of Management Proceedings*, 1977.

Glueck, W., and R. Willis. "Documentary Sources and Strategic Management." *Academy of Management Review* 4 (1979): 95-102.

Hammermesh, R. G., M. J. Anderson, Jr., and J. E. Harris. "Strategies for Low Market Share Businesses." *Harvard Business Review*, May-June 1978, pp. 95-102.

Hofer, C. "Toward a Contingency Theory of Business Strategy." *Academy of Management Journal*, December 1975, pp. 784-810.

Hofer, C., and D. Schendel. *Strategy Formulation: Analytical Concepts*. St. Paul, Minn.: West.

Kent, C., D. Sexton, and K. Vesper. *Encyclopedia of Entrepreneurship*. Englewood Cliffs, N.J.: Prentice-Hall, 1982.

Kuhn, R. "Creative Decision Making: Categories and Constructs." *Journal of Enterprise Management* (England), in press.

_____. "Decision-making: Intuition or Analysis?" *Texas Business*, March 1983, pp. 21-23.

_____. "Get on with Cross-Pollination." *Texas Business*, January 1983, pp. 8-9.

_____. "Hands across the Interface." *Texas Business*, June 1982, p. 46.

_____. *Mid-sized Firms: Success Strategies and Methodologies*. New York: Praeger, 1982.

_____ . "Partners in Profit." *Texas Business*, April 1982, pp. 112-18.

_____ . "Small Companies, Get off the Dole!" *Texas Business*, May 1982, pp. 6-7.

_____ . "Testing Your EQ." *Texas Business*, December 1982, p. 23.

_____ . "Winds of Change." *Texas Business*, December 1982, pp. 65-67.

_____ , ed. *Commercializing Defense-Related Technology*. New York: Praeger, forthcoming.

Kvasha, Y. "Concentration of Production and Small-Scale Industry." *Voprosy Ekonomiki*, May 1967, pp. 26-31. Translated in U.S., Congress, *Hearings on Economic Concentrations*, Cong. sess., pt. 7A: 4358-62.

Lauenstein, M. C., and W. Skinner. "Formulating a Strategy of Superior Resources." *Journal of Business Strategy* 1 (Summer 1980): 4-10.

Liao, S. "The Effects of the Size of Firms on Managerial Attitude." *California Management Review*, Winter 1975, pp. 59-65.

McClelland, D. *Motivating Economic Achievement*. New York: Free Press, 1969.

_____ . "Need Achievement and Entrepreneurship: A Longitudinal Study." *Journal of Personality and Social Psychology*, 1965.

Mancuso, J. R. *Fun 'n' Guts, The Entrepreneur's Philosophy*. Reading, Mass.: Addison-Wesley, 1977.

_____ . *How to Start, Finance, and Manage Your Own Small Business*. Englewood Cliffs, N.J.: Prentice-Hall, 1978.

Marcus, M. "Profitability and Size of Firm." *Review of Economics and Statistics*, February 1969, pp. 104-7.

Mueller, D. "A Life Cycle Theory of the Firm." *Journal of Industrial Economics*, July 1972, pp. 199-219.

Porter, M., and Z. Zannetos. "Administrative Regulation versus Market Regulation in the Diversified Firm." *MIT Working Paper*, April 1978, pp. 978-87.

Roberts, E. B. "Entrepreneurship and Technology." *Research Management*, July 1968.

Roberts, E. B., and H. A. Wainer. "Some Characteristics of Technical Entrepreneurs." *I.E.E.E. Transactions on Engineering Management*, vol. EM-18, no. 3, 1971.

Ronstadt, R., and R. J. Kramer. "Internationalizing Industrial Innovation." *Journal of Business Strategy* 3 (Winter 1983): 3-15.

Rumelt, R. *Strategy, Structure, and Economic Performance*. Boston: Harvard Business School Division of Research, 1974.

Samuels, J., and D. Smyth. "Profits, Variability of Profits and Firm Size." *Economica*, May 1968, pp. 127-40.

Sexton, D. L. "Characteristics and Role Demands of Successful Entrepreneurs." *Academy of Management Proceedings*, 1980.

Schendel, D., and C. Hofer. *Strategic Management*. Boston: Little, Brown, 1979.

Scherer, F. M. *Industrial Market Structure and Economic Performance*. Chicago: Rand McNally, 1980.

Shapero, A., and L. Sokol. "The Social Dimensions of Entrepreneurship." In *Encyclopedia of Entrepreneurship*, edited by C. Kent, D. Sexton, and K. Vesper. Englewood Cliffs, N.J.: Prentice-Hall, 1982.

Shepherd, William G. *The Economics of Industrial Organization*. Englewood Cliffs, N.J.: Prentice-Hall, 1979.

Staw, B., ed. *Psychological Foundations of Organizational Behavior*. Santa Monica, Calif.: Goodyear, 1977.

Steiner, Gary A. *The Creative Organization*. Chicago: University of Chicago Press, 1965.

Steiner, George A. *Strategic Planning*. New York: Macmillan, 1979.

Vesper, K. H. *New Venture Strategies*. Englewood Cliffs, N.J.: Prentice-Hall, 1980.

Woodward, H. "Management Strategies for Small Companies." *Harvard Business Review*, January-February 1976, pp. 113-21.

Zaleznik, A., and M. Kets de Vries. *Power and the Corporate Mind*. Boston: Houghton Mifflin, 1975.

## Chapter 2

# Sources of Capital
# for Very Small Businesses

Robert A. Peterson
and Gerald Albaum

## INTRODUCTION

The concept "robust companies and the entrepreneurial spirit" has broad meaning in that it is applicable to many types of companies. A robust company is one that is healthy, strong, and vigorous. Although the term *entrepreneur* has a somewhat benign definition — "one who organizes, manages, and assumes the risk of a business or enterprise" — common usage of the term adds dimensions of excitement, activity, and newness. Consequently, *entrepreneurial spirit* seems to connote a situation (that is, an environment) in which progress is the norm and stagnancy is not permitted. There is a sense of innovativeness attached to entrepreneurs; the *practice of entrepreneurship* is frequently considered synonymous with *small business*, either newly formed ventures or existing companies that have been purchased and redirected. In either instance, there is typically something "new" involved — a new product, a new service, a new technology, a new idea, or a new structure.

This chapter is concerned with the behavior of "very small" businesses — those with ten or fewer employees. It is this segment of small business that is most often associated with entrepreneurial activity. Specifically, the primary purpose of this chapter is to report the results of two surveys conducted in 1982 by the Institute for Constructive Capitalism at the University of Texas at Austin regarding the sources of investment capital and operating capital of very small businesses. Before doing so, however, a general perspective is provided on these businesses – the problems they face and the concerns they have.

## THE NATURE OF SMALL BUSINESS

### Importance

Small business is an essential component of the U.S. economic system, which has been characterized as a two-tiered structure of small businesses and large corporations (Walker and Wooten, 1980; Chandran, DeSalvia, and Young, 1977). Indeed, in a 1982 report to Congress, President Ronald Reagan stated that "small business is the heart and soul of our free enterprise system" (*The State of Small Business: A Report of the President*, 1982, p. 20).

There is no consensus as to how a small business should be defined. For example, the Small Business Administration (SBA) considers businesses with less than 500 employees to be small, although many individuals would argue that a firm with 500 employees is no longer small. Even so, it is generally agreed that small businesses are important to the economy in terms of number of firms, employment, innovations, and the many products and services provided. Using the SBA criterion, 99.8 percent of the businesses in the United States are small; collectively these businesses employ 47 percent of the nongovernment labor force and produce 38 percent of the nation's private domestic product (U.S. Small Business Administration, 1982, p. 2). Using a more restrictive, employment-based definition of *small business*, nine out of ten businesses have fewer than 10 employees, businesses with less than 20 employees create two of every three new jobs, and about 80 percent of all new jobs are created by firms with 100 or fewer employees (Thoryn, 1982, p. 40).

Or, consider the following. While no precise count currently exists of businesses with ten or fewer employees, a reasonable estimate drawn from *The State of Small Business: A Report of the President* (1982) is that a minimum of 8.4 million such businesses fall into this category. Conservatively assuming four as the typical number of employees, and that each employee's family averages 2.8 members, this means that some 94 million Americans are directly impacted by the fate of businesses with ten or fewer employees.

Moreover, it has been estimated that small businesses are generally more than two times as innovative per employee as large businesses (U.S. Small Business Administration, 1982, p. 5). Whether this innovations-per-employee ratio can be generalized to the extent that small businesses are, in the aggregate, more innovative than large businesses remains an open question. Indeed, there are many who believe otherwise. Gorb (1980), for example, has stated:

> That small businesses are generally more innovating than large ones is also highly unlikely. No one has reliable information either way, but many new innovative start-ups certainly derive from ideas which originated (and were paid for) in large companies and which an enterprising individual (usually a middle manager) has taken away to implement through a new small business. [p. 265]
>
> This process, entrepreneurial rather than innovative, is a commendable one. Indeed, it is being encouraged nowadays by many large firms who call it . . . "spin off" and see it as a way of developing a process or idea, which for many reasons may have a low priority for the larger firm. [p. 266]

Likewise, more than a quarter of a century ago, Galbraith (1956) predicted the demise of the independent inventor and small business as a viable force in technological innovation:

> Most of the cheap and simple inventions have, to put it bluntly and unpersuasively, been made. . . . Because development is costly, it follows that it can be carried on only by a firm that has the resources which are associated with considerable size. [pp. 86-87]

Despite such pessimistic views, there is continued evidence that many large businesses have proved to be not particularly innovative and that independent entrepreneurs and inventors in small businesses still appear to be contributing many innovative technological breakthroughs (Hawkins, 1976). In turn, these innovations have been the foundation of many new small businesses.

In brief, small businesses play an important, useful, and absolutely essential role in the economy in that they:

1.  Provide a production outlet for the energies of enterprising and energetic people.

2. Act as specialist suppliers — producing parts, subassemblies or components at a lower cost than possible for large firms.
3. Add to the variety of products and services in the market place.
4. Check monopoly profits and the inefficiency which a monopoly might breed.
5. Are a source of innovation in products, services and techniques.
6. Breed new industries and new sources of employment.
7. Provide a seed bed for new entrepreneurial talent and a base for new companies to grow and challenge established leaders. [Chandran, DeSalvia, and Young, 1977, p. 31]

## Characteristics of Small Businesses

Although knowledge of the economic importance of small business is useful, by itself it only provides a partial picture. For a comprehensive perspective, it is also necessary to recognize the unique characteristics of small businesses and understand how they differ from large businesses.

Traditionally, small businesses have been unable to compete directly in highly concentrated manufacturing industries. Therefore, they have remained primarily in the service, construction, wholesaling, and retailing sectors of the economy. Those small businesses that do enter the manufacturing sector tend to have products based on narrow skills and an abbreviated product mix, and their products tend to be susceptible to obsolescence and technological change (Chandran, DeSalvia, and Young, 1977). This last point, of course, reflects their relative concentration in high technology industries.

Small business is different from large business. To illustrate: compared with large businesses, small businesses have higher sales per dollar of assets and fewer assets per employee. While this is in part a function of the industries in which they typically operate (for example, services), it also relates to the major distinguishing feature between large and small businesses: *resource poverty*. According to Welsh and White (1981), resource poverty comes about because:

1. Small business tends to be clustered in relatively fragmented industries — e.g., wholesaling, retailing, services, job shop manufacturing — that have many competitors who are not adverse to building revenues and share-of-market by cutting prices.

2. The owner-manager's salary is a relatively large proportion of revenues.

3. External forces tend to have more impact on small businesses than on large businesses. Changes in government regulations, tax laws, labor and interest rates generally affect a greater percentage of costs for small businesses than for large businesses. [p. 18]

Consequently, a small business must build its organization around its key resource(s), be it a specific technology, a unique material, an advantageous location, or the talents of its owner-manager. It must often make do with what it has, since it possesses limited access to both financial and managerial resources. These conditions, together with the specific problems and concerns facing small business, collectively require management approaches different from those appropriate in large businesses. In the next section, selected issues for small business are overviewed.*

## PROBLEMS FACING SMALL BUSINESS

Insights into the problems faced by small businesses can be obtained from a variety of sources. It may be possible, for example, to investigate the primary causes of small business failures by analyzing the characteristics of failed firms.† Another approach is to survey small business people regarding their perceptions as to why small businesses fail. In a recent study, Peterson, Kozmetsky, and Ridgway (1983) report that owners and managers of small business firms perceived "lack of management expertise," which includes lack of financial expertise and knowledge, to be the primary cause of small business failures. As shown in Table 2-1, in addition to this cause and general causes related to the economy, other perceived causes of small business failures were high interest rates, undercapitalization, and cash flow.

The significance of the financial dimension as a major cause of small business failures has been aptly summarized by Wucinich (1979):

---

*For different views on such management approaches, see Tibbits (1979), Welsh and White (1981), and Green (1982).

†See, for example, Brockhaus (1980), Petrof (1980), and Brockhaus and Nord (1979).

**Table 2-1**

Perceived Primary Cause of Small Business Failures

|  | Percentage Response | | |
|---|---|---|---|
| *Cause* | *Total Sample* | *Managers* | *Owners* |
| Lack of management expertise | 29.1 | 27.9 | 29.6 |
| High interest rates | 15.6 | 11.5 | 17.7 |
| Recession/economy/inflation/ unemployment | 11.4 | 13.1 | 11.1 |
| Undercapitalization/overextension | 10.1 | 6.1 | 11.7 |
| Taxes | 5.8 | 6.7 | 5.2 |
| Competition | 5.8 | 7.4 | 4.9 |
| Cash flow | 5.0 | 6.1 | 4.9 |
| Federal regulations | 3.6 | 4.5 | 3.5 |
| High overhead | 2.5 | 2.6 | 2.1 |
| Other | 11.1 | 14.1 | 9.3 |
| Total | 100.0 | 100.0 | 100.0 |

*Source*: Peterson, Kozmetsky, and Ridgway, 1983, p. 7.

Two basic problems facing owners of most small companies [are] a need for capital and lack of financial expertise and knowledge required to determine the firm's financial needs.

Insufficient financing is a major cause of small business failure. In fact, Dun and Bradstreet ranks it as one of the nine major pitfalls of managing a small business. A lack of financial understanding and planning may cause the small entrepreneur to apply for an incorrect amount of funds or perhaps obtain the wrong type of financing. [p. 16]

In general, financial problems are among the most important problems, if not the single most important problem, facing small businesses in the 1980s. Three studies can be used to corroborate this conclusion. First, in early 1982, *INC.* Magazine contained a discussion of a survey of its subscribers who were asked to indicate their three most important concerns. As shown in Table 2-2, by far the most important concern was interest rates. Also included among the 24 concerns were availability of long-term and short-term credit

**Table 2-2**

Most Important Economic Concerns to Small Business
in 1982

| Factor | Weighted Score* |
|---|---|
| Interest rates | 192 |
| Growth of the economy | 48 |
| Availability of long-term credit | 40 |
| Ability to pass on price increases | 40 |
| Availability of short-term credit | 38 |
| Wage costs | 29 |
| Energy costs | 25 |
| Raw materials costs | 22 |
| Quality of labor | 21 |
| Federal taxes | 19 |
| Domestic competition | 18 |
| Regulatory environment | 15 |
| Federal spending | 14 |
| Availability of equity capital | 12 |
| Availability of labor | 8 |
| Foreign competition | 8 |
| State/local taxes | 8 |
| Government aid for small business | 7 |
| State/local spending | 6 |
| Stock and bond markets | 5 |
| Mergers and takeovers | 5 |
| Supply of energy | 4 |
| Union activity | 4 |
| Foreign exchange rates | 4 |

*Computed by giving a weight of 3 to the percentage of times listed first, 2 to the times listed second, and 1 to the times listed third.

*Source*: "What's Going to Happen in '82?" 1982, p. 32.

as well as availability of equity capital. Second, the National Federation of Independent Businesses (NFIB) conducts a quarterly survey
of its membership to determine major problems and concerns. The
April 1982 survey indicated that survey respondents considered
interest rates and financing their most important problem. And 37
percent of the NFIB members surveyed reported this to be a serious
problem. In fact, since July 1981 this problem has surpassed inflation as the single most important problem facing small business each
time the NFIB has conducted its survey.*

The third illustration is drawn from a recent study by Albaum,
Peterson, and Kozmetsky (1983), who surveyed small business
owners and managers twice within a six-month period and asked
the following open-end question: "What is the *single* most important
problem facing *your business* at the present time?"

Summary results for this question are presented in Table 2-3.
From the table it is apparent that while a variety of responses were
obtained, in both surveys the most frequently cited problems related
to the recession and low demand faced by the survey respondents'
businesses. The next most frequently cited problems were financial
in nature — cash flow as well as cost and availability of capital.
For the most part, responses were relatively consistent across the
two surveys as well as across sample subgroups, although interesting
observations can be made. Cost and availability of money declined
somewhat from the first to the second survey as a reported problem, partially owing to the lowering of interest rates over the time
period between the surveys.

In addition, owners, as contrasted with managers, were more
prone to perceive their most important problem as being financial-
or personnel-related, most likely reflecting their particular managerial responsibilities. A greater percentage of owners than managers
(about a 10 percentage point difference in both surveys) indicated
that cash flow, cost of money, rising costs, or personnel problems
was the single most important problem they faced. To a large extent,
this difference reflects the perceptions of owners who started their
business themselves rather than purchasing an ongoing concern.
Finally, as would be expected, cash flow was cited relatively more

---

*Any interpretation of these concerns and problems must obviously take
into account the *timing* of the surveys. Both took place during a period of
exceedingly high interest rates and low capital availability.

**Table 2-3**
Single Most Important Problem Facing Small Businesses

| Problem | Percentage Response | |
| --- | --- | --- |
| | *August 1982* | *February 1983* |
| Economy/recession/inflation/ | | |
| unemployment | 18.7 | 19.0 |
| Low demand | 22.9 | 24.5 |
| Cash flow | 14.0 | 13.2 |
| Overburdened/paperwork | 1.4 | 1.3 |
| Cost of money/interest rates/ | | |
| availability of money | 11.1 | 7.7 |
| Government regulations | 1.4 | 1.7 |
| Specific costs rising | 3.9 | 4.2 |
| Untrained labor/personnel problems | 6.5 | 3.2 |
| Other | 12.2 | 13.7 |
| No problems | 7.9 | 11.5 |
| Total | 100.0 | 100.0 |

*Source*: Albaum, Peterson, and Kozmetsky, 1983.

frequently as a problem by survey participants from product-based businesses than by survey participants from service-based businesses.

## Financial Considerations

Despite the obvious importance of financing to the survival and growth of small businesses (illustrated in part by the above), relatively little empirical research on the topic has been reported in the literature. In a study limited to small businesses in six southeastern states, Shih (1982) presented the results of examining the range of financial resources available to small business. Specifically, survey participants were asked what financial services they had used in the previous five years and the source of each service. However, no distinction was made between operating capital and investment (start-up or expansion) capital in her study. Another regional study (in five southwestern states) examined small businesses' credit and venture capital requirements and their sources of funding (Shatto, 1981). Additional insight was sought by surveying commercial banks in one of the states.

Recently, Eisemann and Andrews (1981) investigated alternative sources of debt financing available to small businesses and the role of commercial banks in the debt financing process. Two conclusions reached were that — with respect to extended funding — small businesses rely on debt financing to a greater extent than equity financing and that commercial banks, while an important source of discretionary borrowing, are not the major source of debt financing for small businesses. Finally, a study of small manufacturers reported that internally generated equity and commercial banks were the only two sources of financing predominant in the financial structure of small businesses, and this was true for both initial (start-up) and growth (operating) financing (Jones, 1979).

In brief, there is no shortage of experientially based or case study-based discussions of sources of financing for small business.* Simultaneously though, it is quite evident that there are still major gaps in what is known about small business financing activities and needs. These gaps exist as a consequence of a lack, per se, of empirically based expositions; of those that do exist, nearly all are derived from small, regional convenience samples. Additionally, there is a virtual absence of published information documenting the sources of capital utilized by very small businesses — those with ten or fewer employees. The remainder of this chapter is an attempt to provide generalizable information on the sources of capital used by businesses with ten or fewer employees.

## THE PRESENT STUDY

As previously mentioned, this chapter reports selected results from two surveys conducted by the Institute for Constructive Capitalism during the last five months of 1982. These surveys generally explored broad issues facing small businesses in the United States, although this chapter only reports findings pertaining to sources of original

---

*See, for example, "Financing for Small Business Clients" (1980), "Where Does Growth Money Come From?" (1978), Patrick (1980), Shatto (1980), Goldman (1979), Rollins (1979), and Swadener (1976).

investment capital and operating capital. The two surveys are related in that the results of the first served as input to, and the foundation of, the second.

## Telephone Survey

The general research approach used in the first survey consisted of collecting requisite data from a national sample of one particular small business segment — businesses employing ten or fewer employees — by means of telephone interviews. All interviews were conducted from a single, supervised telephone room, using professional interviewers. Interviews were conducted during a two-week period in August 1982 on weekdays between the hours of 11:00 A.M. and 5:00 P.M. A minimum of two call-backs was made for each telephone number when contact was not made on the initial attempt. The interviewing process was validated in part by a listen-in technique and in part by supervisors re-calling 10 percent of the individuals interviewed.

The sampling frame consisted of a list of approximately 4,400 businesses in the 48 contiguous states obtained from a national list company. This list was a random sample of businesses whose net worth was less than $200,000.

Each of the businesses contained in the sampling frame was telephoned, with the interviewer asking to speak to the owner or manager, at which time the potential survey participant was questioned as to whether the business employed ten or fewer people (including the potential respondent). Owners or managers in businesses meeting this criterion who agreed to participate in the survey were then asked a series of questions about issues relevant to small businesses.

Three questions were directed only to owners and inquired into sources of investment and operating capital. In particular, the following three open-end questions were posed to survey participants who owned their business: "*Where* did you get the capital or money to buy or start this business?" "*What other* sources of capital or money did you have when you bought or started this business?" "*Where* are you currently getting your operating capital or money you need to continue in business?" Responses to these questions were initially subjected to a content analysis to determine the most frequently given answers. These answers were then assigned numerical codes, which were used for categorizing and analyzing the survey data.

Data were provided by the owners or managers of 1,001 small businesses.* Each of the 48 contiguous states was represented in the final sample obtained such that the sample size was large enough and sufficiently geographically diverse to allow generalization within the context of the research process used. The number of completed interviews per state ranged from 1 in Montana to 85 in California and Texas each.

Table 2-4 presents selected characteristics of the sample. About two thirds of the survey participants, 670, owned their small business. These individuals served as the analysis base for the present investigation. Of these small business owners, 71 percent reported starting a new business rather than purchasing an existing one. Approximately one half of the 670 businesses sampled were sole

**Table 2-4**

Dispositions of Samples in Telephone and Mail Surveys

| | Percentage Response | |
|---|---|---|
| Characteristic | Telephone Survey | Mail Survey |
| Owner-manager | | |
| Manager | 33.0 | 9.9 |
| Owner | 67.0 | 90.1 |
| Business formation (owners) | | |
| Purchased business | 28.9 | 32.9 |
| Started business | 71.1 | 67.1 |
| Business organization (owners) | | |
| Sole Proprietorship | 46.5 | 18.1 |
| Partnership | 12.6 | 3.6 |
| Corporation | 40.9 | 78.3 |

*Source*: Compiled by the author.

---

*In addition to a large number of businesses not meeting the number of employees criterion, numerous businesses contained in the sampling frame were no longer in existence. There were also 64 interview terminations.

proprietorships, while another 40 percent were corporations. Because of the great diversity of the businesses, no attempt was made to definitively categorize their industry or primary product or service offering. It is apparent, however, that the majority of the businesses sampled were retail related.

## Mail Survey

In the second survey, data were collected by means of mail interviews. Traditional mail survey research techniques and procedures were employed when collecting the data, including the mailing of a follow-up questionnaire to initial nonrespondents. Analogous to the telephone survey, this survey was concerned with small business issues in addition to sources of investment and operating capital. However, also analogous to the telephone survey, only those findings relevant to the topic of sources of investment and operating capital are reported here.

The original sample consisted of 1,997 small businesses that were randomly selected from the customer list of a New York Stock Exchange firm that specializes in marketing products and services to small businesses. This initial sample represented less than 1 percent of the company's customers (typically described as service-oriented businesses with five to six employees).

Questionnaires were mailed to the owners of the businesses sampled in November 1982. Responses were received from 353 individuals; this represents an effective response rate of 19.4 percent since 174 questionnaires were returned by the U.S. Post Office as undeliverable. Small businesses contained in the sample were located in 22 states (all east of the Rocky Mountains) and Washington, D.C., and reflect the customer composition of the company providing the sampling frame. The number of completed questionnaires per state ranged from 1 in Nebraska and Missouri each to 66 in Pennsylvania. Most major Standard Industrial Code (SIC) categories are represented in the sample. As Table 2-4 indicates, more than 90 percent of the individuals responding were small business owners. Only the questionnaire answers of these 318 owners were analyzed in the present investigation.

Other relevant characteristics of the mail survey sample are also reported in Table 2-4. Approximately two thirds of the responding small business owners started their business. More than three fourths of the firms represented were corporations, while slightly less than 20 percent were sole proprietorships.

With respect to the topic of interest, sources of capital, owners were asked to respond to two constant sum scales (Peterson, 1982, pp. 286-87) that included prespecified sources of capital that could be used to start or operate their business:

Below are sources of *investment capital* (money used to start or purchase a business). In each space provided, indicate the percentage of investment capital obtained from each source that was used to *start* or *purchase* your business. Be sure that the percentages add to 100%.

\_\_\_\_\_% Personal Savings
\_\_\_\_\_% Sale of Personal Assets
\_\_\_\_\_% Investment Capital from Family Members
\_\_\_\_\_% Short-term Bank Loan (maturity less than one year)
\_\_\_\_\_% Long-term Bank Loan (maturity greater than one year)
\_\_\_\_\_% Small Business Administration Guaranteed Loan
\_\_\_\_\_% Individual Investors not in Family
\_\_\_\_\_% Venture Capital Firm
\_\_\_\_\_% Other _____ (Please Specify)
\_\_\_\_\_% Other _____ (Please Specify)

  100 % Total

and

Below are sources of *operating capital* (money used to meet current payments to keep the business going). In each space provided, indicate the percentage of operating capital obtained from each source which is used to *operate* your business. Be sure that the percentages add to 100%.

\_\_\_\_\_% Short-term Bank Loan (maturity less than one year)
\_\_\_\_\_% Deposits or Prepayments
\_\_\_\_\_% Rents or Earnings from Other Business Activities
\_\_\_\_\_% Reinvested Earnings (profits)
\_\_\_\_\_% Sales of Accounts Receivable to a Financial Institution
\_\_\_\_\_% Other _____ (Please Specify)
\_\_\_\_\_% Other _____ (Please Specify)

## SOURCES OF CAPITAL

Because the two surveys provided data about small business segments that are somewhat different from each other, results are provided separately for each survey. Taken together, though, the two surveys provide a broad perspective on the sources of investment and operating capital used by very small businesses.

### Telephone Survey Results

Tables 2-5 and 2-6, respectively, present responses to the two open-end questions inquiring into the sources that small business owners in the telephone survey used to obtain investment capital when starting or purchasing their business. From the tables it is initially apparent that only 41 percent of the owners used more than a single source for their investment capital and that owners of sole proprietorships were more likely to use only a single source for their capital than were owners whose businesses were organized as either partnerships or corporations.

Table 2-5 reveals that the primary source of investment capital was internally generated or "self" — personal savings, insurance cash value, or assets obtained from a prior business. Nearly six out of ten owners stated that their investment capital was internally generated. When responses to the "second most important source of investment capital" question are considered (Table 2-6), approximately two thirds of the owners surveyed, 65 percent, indicated that "self" was either their primary or secondary source of investment capital.

An additional 20 percent of the owners surveyed stated their primary source of investment capital was either bank credit or a bank loan. Other answers given included "sold assets or took out a mortgage" (7 percent) and "equity from relatives or friends" (6 percent). Only 1 percent of the small business owners stated that they obtained their initial investment capital from "company headquarters." (These businesses were essentially franchises.) An additional 1 percent of the small business owners reported obtaining an SBA loan. Although the finding that SBA loans were relatively unimportant is not unexpected since the SBA is a "lender of last resort," the percentage of firms using this type of financing is less

## Table 2-5
### Primary Source of Investment Capital
(percentage response)

| Source | Total Sample of Owners | Business Formation | | Business Organization | | |
| --- | --- | --- | --- | --- | --- | --- |
| | | Purchased Business | Started Business | Sole Proprietorship | Partnership | Corporation |
| Self-savings/insurance/ prior business | 57.4 | 44.6 | 63.3 | 57.3 | 60.2 | 56.3 |
| Bank credit or loan | 20.4 | 25.1 | 18.3 | 20.3 | 20.4 | 20.9 |
| Sold assets/mortgage | 6.8 | 12.8 | 4.5 | 6.3 | 7.5 | 7.4 |
| Investor equity | 1.9 | 3.1 | 1.2 | 1.3 | 3.2 | 2.3 |
| Company headquarters | 1.2 | 1.5 | 0.8 | 1.1 | 0.0 | 1.4 |
| SBA loan | 1.0 | 0.0 | 1.4 | 1.3 | 1.2 | 0.5 |
| Equity from relatives or friends | 6.4 | 6.2 | 6.6 | 8.2 | 3.2 | 4.7 |
| Other | 4.9 | 6.7 | 3.9 | 4.2 | 4.3 | 6.5 |
| Total | 100.0 | 100.0 | 100.0 | 100.0 | 100.0 | 100.0 |

SBA = Small Business Administration
*Source*: Telephone survey.

38

**Table 2-6**
Secondary Source of Investment Capital
(percentage response)

| Source | Total Sample of Owners | Business Formation | | Business Organization | | |
|---|---|---|---|---|---|---|
| | | Purchased Business | Started Business | Sole Proprietorship | Partnership | Corporation |
| Income | 4.0 | 3.7 | 4.0 | 5.4 | 3.3 | 1.4 |
| Dividends from other investments | 1.6 | 2.6 | 1.3 | 2.2 | 1.1 | 1.0 |
| Pension/retirement fund/ insurance | 0.9 | 1.0 | 0.8 | 0.5 | 2.2 | 1.0 |
| Land/mortgage/other assets | 4.9 | 4.7 | 5.2 | 3.5 | 6.6 | 6.7 |
| Savings | 13.1 | 16.8 | 11.2 | 11.9 | 7.7 | 17.2 |
| Bank credit or loan | 12.3 | 14.7 | 11.4 | 9.5 | 19.8 | 14.4 |
| Other | 4.6 | 6.3 | 3.8 | 3.8 | 5.5 | 5.7 |
| None | 58.6 | 50.2 | 62.3 | 63.2 | 53.8 | 52.6 |
| Total | 100.0 | 100.0 | 100.0 | 100.0 | 100.0 | 100.0 |

*Source*: Telephone survey.

than might be expected, given publicity surrounding, and awareness of, the SBA loan program.

Although source of investment capital did not differ appreciably by type of business organization, there were source differences as a function of whether owners started their business or purchased an existing business. Given the nature of small business start-ups, it is not surprising that a relatively greater proportion of the owners who started a new business used personal funds than did those owners purchasing an existing business. This difference undoubtedly reflects the relative difficulty of obtaining funds from financial institutions (as well as the high cost of such funds) when starting a new business because of the risk involved.

A slightly different perspective on the sources of investment capital used can be obtained by examining the combination of sources used. Table 2-7 reveals the relative frequencies with which certain combinations of investment sources were used by the owners surveyed. More than 40 percent of the owners financed their business *only* through a self-funding or internal mechanism. Indeed, a majority of the owners' investment capital was obtained from only two sources: "self" and "bank loans."

Survey participants in the telephone survey were also queried concerning their current source of operating capital. As Table 2-8 indicates, a substantial majority of the owners surveyed, 72 percent, stated that "profits" was their major source of operating capital. The next most frequently cited source was "credit/bank

**Table 2-7**
Major Sources of Investment Capital

| Source | Percentage of Sample Using |
|---|---|
| Self only | 40.6 |
| Self and bank loan | 14.6 |
| Bank loan only | 11.3 |
| Other source/combinations | 33.5 |

*Source*: Telephone survey.

**Table 2-8**

**Current Source of Operating Capital**

(percentage response)

| Source | Total Sample of Owners | Business Formation | | Business Organization | | |
|---|---|---|---|---|---|---|
| | | Purchased Business | Started Business | Sole Proprietorship | Partnership | Corporation |
| Profits | 72.4 | 74.2 | 77.3 | 75.8 | 76.6 | 67.8 |
| Credit/bank loans | 15.5 | 19.3 | 14.8 | 15.1 | 12.1 | 17.0 |
| New equity | 1.0 | 0.0 | 0.6 | 0.4 | 1.6 | 1.0 |
| Receivables/inventor/ prepayment | 0.7 | 0.6 | 0.8 | 0.4 | 0.0 | 1.2 |
| State or federal loans | 0.2 | 0.0 | 0.0 | 0.0 | 0.0 | 0.6 |
| Income from other businesses | 1.6 | 0.7 | 1.6 | 1.5 | 1.6 | 1.7 |
| Company headquarters | 2.3 | 0.7 | 0.2 | 0.2 | 2.4 | 4.7 |
| Other | 3.4 | 2.9 | 3.7 | 4.4 | 1.6 | 2.7 |
| None | 1.0 | 1.6 | 1.0 | 1.1 | 0.8 | 0.7 |
| Don't know | 1.9 | 0.0 | 0.0 | 1.1 | 3.3 | 2.6 |
| Total | 100.0 | 100.0 | 100.0 | 100.0 | 100.0 | 100.0 |

*Source*: Telephone survey.

41

loans"; 16 percent of the owners indicated that this was their major source of operating capital. In general, corporations were less likely than sole proprietorships or partnerships to use profits as a source of operating capital. Interestingly enough, though, with one exception there was no systematic relationship between source of investment capital and source of operating capital. The exception was bank loans. While 16 percent of the total sample used bank loans as a source of operating capital, 27 percent of the owners using a bank loan as a source of investment capital also used it as a source of operating capital.

## Mail Survey Results*

The findings of the telephone study provided a foundation as well as a direction for a more in-depth examination, by means of a mail survey, of sources of investment and operating capital. As previously noted, in the mail survey small business owners were asked to indicate the percentage of investment capital obtained from each of eight prespecified sources.

Table 2-9 reveals that the most frequently used source of investment capital was personal savings. Almost three quarters of the owners surveyed reported that they used personal savings when starting or purchasing their business. Other sources of investment capital used by more than one quarter of the responding owners included long-term bank loans (27 percent) and family members (26 percent). Not only were these three the most frequently used sources, but they also accounted for the greatest shares of investment capital. On the average, for *all* owners surveyed, more than 43 percent of the owners' investment capital came from personal savings, 17 percent was derived from long-term bank loans, and 12 percent was obtained from family members. If only the owners actually using personal savings as a source are considered, the percentage of investment capital accounted for by personal savings rises

*Appreciation is expressed to Robert Walston for his assistance in this survey. Portions of the results presented here have been previously discussed in his professional report, "Analysis of the Opinions and Attitudes on Issues Confronting Small Businesses with Ten or Fewer Employees."

# Table 2-9
## Sources of Investment Capital

| Source | Total Sample of Owners | | Business Formation | | | | Business Organization | | | | | |
|---|---|---|---|---|---|---|---|---|---|---|---|---|
| | | | Purchased Business | | Started Business | | Sole Proprietorship | | Partnership | | Corporation | |
| | Percentage Using | Mean Percentage of Total Investment Capital | Percentage Using | Mean Percentage of Total Investment Capital | Percentage Using | Mean Percentage of Total Investment Capital | Percentage Using | Mean Percentage of Total Investment Capital | Percentage Using | Mean Percentage of Total Investment Capital | Percentage Using | Mean Percentage of Total Investment Capital |
| Personal savings | 73.7 | 43.4 | 72.0 | 33.6 | 74.5 | 49.2 | 70.7 | 38.7 | 76.9 | 43.7 | 73.2 | 44.6 |
| Sale of personal assets | 14.8 | 5.6 | 17.0 | 4.6 | 14.7 | 6.4 | 17.2 | 6.6 | 7.7 | 0.9 | 14.6 | 5.6 |
| Family | 25.9 | 12.2 | 29.0 | 12.4 | 23.0 | 9.9 | 20.7 | 10.7 | 23.1 | 10.0 | 27.2 | 12.6 |
| Short-term bank loan | 15.5 | 7.0 | 11.0 | 6.3 | 18.1 | 7.5 | 19.0 | 10.8 | 7.7 | 7.9 | 15.0 | 6.0 |
| Long-term bank loan | 26.8 | 16.6 | 38.0 | 25.7 | 21.6 | 12.0 | 32.8 | 19.8 | 23.1 | 14.7 | 25.6 | 15.9 |
| SBA loan | 3.2 | 2.0 | 2.0 | 1.3 | 3.9 | 2.4 | 3.4 | 2.3 | 7.7 | 6.3 | 2.8 | 1.7 |
| Outside investors | 10.7 | 5.0 | 10.0 | 4.6 | 11.8 | 5.5 | 6.9 | 3.2 | 7.7 | 2.7 | 11.8 | 5.6 |
| Venture capital firms | 1.3 | 0.9 | 0.0 | 0.0 | 2.0 | 1.4 | 1.7 | 0.3 | 0.0 | 0.0 | 1.2 | 1.1 |
| Other* | 10.4 | 7.3 | 17.0 | 11.5 | 7.8 | 5.7 | 8.6 | 7.6 | 15.4 | 13.8 | 10.6 | 6.9 |
| Total | | 100.0 | | 100.0 | | 100.0 | | 100.0 | | 100.0 | | 100.0 |

SBA = Small Business Administration

*Includes previous-owner financed, loans from family and friends, and so on.

*Source*: Mail survey.

to nearly 59 percent, a figure that corresponds rather closely to that obtained in the telephone survey.

Perusal of Table 2-9 reveals that the type of business organization did not have a statistically significant effect upon either the incidence of use or extent of use of any of the eight sources investigated. How the small business was founded, though, did affect the extent of use of personal savings and both the incidence and the extent of use of long-term bank loans. Owners starting small businesses tended to use personal savings to a greater extent than did owners who purchased their business. For the former, 49 percent of their investment capital came from personal savings, whereas for the latter group almost 34 percent of their investment capital came from personal savings. With respect to long-term bank loans, 38 percent of those purchasing a business reported using such a loan, while almost 22 percent of the owners starting a new business reported using this investment capital source. Moreover, the mean percentages of investment capital derived from long-term bank loans varied from 12 percent for owners starting their business to 26 percent for owners purchasing their business. Considering the eight prespecified sources of investment capital, there is a significant relative relationship between the percentage of owners using a source and the percentage of total capital that the source accounted for ($r_s$ = .9, $p < .01$). Succinctly stated, the larger the percentage of owners utilizing a source, the larger the average percentage of investment capital accounted for by the source.

Table 2-10 shows that about 60 percent of the survey participants used more than one source for their investment capital, with the mean number of sources used being 1.8. Only 4 percent of the owners reported using more than three sources. Number of sources used did not significantly differ as a function of business formation or the manner in which the business was organized.

Using the same format as that employed for the investment capital question, small business owners were asked to indicate the percentage of operating capital obtained from a list of five sources. As shown in Table 2-11, two thirds of the owners relied on reinvested earnings or profits for their operating capital, and this source, on the average, accounted for nearly one half of their operating capital. Other widely used sources included short-term bank loans and deposits/prepayments, although these sources only accounted for about 17 percent each of total operating capital.

**Table 2-10**

Number of Sources Used for Investment Capital

| Number of Sources | Percentage Response* |
|---|---|
| None | 1.9 |
| 1 | 39.1 |
| 2 | 40.4 |
| 3 | 14.5 |
| 4 | 2.5 |
| 5 | 1.6 |
| Total | 100.0 |

*Mean = 1.8 sources.
*Source*: Mail survey.

Table 2-11 further reveals that no statistically significant differences existed in either incidence of source use or extent of operating capital derived from the various sources as a function of type of business formation or business organization. In general, the relationship in relative terms between the incidence of source employment and the percentage of operating capital provided by the source paralleled that obtained for investment capital sources ($r_s$ = .89, $p$ < .01). Hence, across sources, the higher the usage incidence, the larger the percentage of operating capital provided (on average).

Over one half of the owners reported using more than one source for meeting operating capital needs. From Table 2-12, it is apparent that the average number of sources is slightly less than two (1.7 to be precise), nearly identical to the number of sources reported in response to the investment capital question. Similar to investment capital source usage, the number of sources used for operating capital did not vary as a function of type of business formation or business organization.

# Table 2-11
## Sources of Operating Capital

| Source | Total Sample of Owners | | Business Formation | | | | Business Organization | | | | | |
|---|---|---|---|---|---|---|---|---|---|---|---|---|
| | | | Purchased Business | | Started Business | | Sole Proprietorship | | Partnership | | Corporation | |
| | Percentage Using | Mean Percentage of Total Investment Capital | Percentage Using | Mean Percentage of Total Investment Capital | Percentage Using | Mean Percentage of Total Investment Capital | Percentage Using | Mean Percentage of Total Investment Capital | Percentage Using | Mean Percentage of Total Investment Capital | Percentage Using | Mean Percentage of Total Investment Capital |
| Reinvested savings/profits | 65.9 | 49.4 | 61.0 | 45.2 | 67.2 | 51.3 | 65.5 | 52.1 | 61.5 | 36.9 | 65.9 | 49.4 |
| Short-term bank loan | 42.6 | 16.6 | 38.0 | 19.3 | 45.6 | 16.0 | 39.7 | 16.5 | 38.5 | 11.8 | 42.6 | 16.6 |
| Deposits/prepayments | 29.3 | 17.2 | 29.0 | 18.5 | 28.4 | 15.8 | 27.6 | 18.6 | 38.5 | 21.4 | 29.3 | 17.2 |
| Earnings from other business activities | 15.8 | 6.4 | 12.0 | 3.9 | 18.6 | 8.0 | 15.5 | 4.3 | 23.1 | 12.3 | 15.8 | 6.4 |
| Sale of receivables | 6.0 | 3.5 | 4.0 | 2.3 | 6.9 | 3.7 | 1.7 | 0.1 | 15.4 | 9.0 | 6.0 | 3.5 |
| Other* | 13.9 | 6.9 | 17.0 | 10.8 | 12.3 | 5.2 | 13.8 | 8.4 | 23.1 | 8.6 | 13.9 | 6.9 |
| Total | | 100.0 | | 100.0 | | 100.0 | | 100.0 | | 100.0 | | 100.0 |

*Includes personal loans from owner, loans from family and friends, and so on.
*Source*: Mail survey.

**Table 2-12**
Number of Sources Used for Operating Capital

| Number of Sources | Percentage Response* |
|---|---|
| None | 2.9 |
| 1 | 42.6 |
| 2 | 38.5 |
| 3 | 11.0 |
| 4 | 4.4 |
| 5 | 0.6 |
| Total | 100.0 |

*Mean = 1.7 sources.
*Source*: Mail survey.

## SUMMARY AND CONCLUSIONS

The primary purpose of the present investigation was to empirically document the sources from which very small businesses obtain their investment and operating capital. While proper financial management is crucial to the success of a small business, there is a paucity of hard data on such issues as sources of financing. Most of the available information is either anecdotal in nature or based upon case studies or convenience samples.

Despite the fact that the two samples of small business owners investigated possessed somewhat different characteristics, the respective results obtained were relatively convergent. In general, two or fewer sources were used for investment capital, while by far the most widely used source was "self," principally personal savings. The second-most popular source of investment capital was "bank loan." Not surprisingly, small business owners starting their business were significantly less likely to use this source than small business owners purchasing their business. Of the sources investigated, the SBA was one of the least frequently used sources of investment capital.

The most frequently used source of operating capital was "profits" or "reinvested earnings," followed by "short-term bank loans." The typical small business owner sampled utilized two or fewer sources of operating capital.

For both investment and operating capital, therefore, internally generated equity and bank loans were the two predominant sources of capital. As such, the present results reinforce the findings of Jones (1979) in his study of small manufacturers.

Because the two surveys were descriptive rather than explanatory in nature, it was not possible to determine *why* particular sources were used or not used or to determine *why* they were used to the extent they were. Thus the surveys do not permit inferences as to whether, for example, the apparently small reliance on bank loans was a result of deliberate decisions by small business owners (for example, not wanting to pay the high cost of borrowing) or whether they were effectively and systematically being excluded from this source of capital. For investment capital, one might be tempted to infer the former, given the various survey findings obtained. Obviously, further research is needed to determine the explanations underlying the phenomena observed in this investigation.

One conclusion is inescapable, however, and it serves to reaffirm what is universally accepted as a characteristic of small business owners. Like the pioneers of old, they are extremely self-reliant and depend primarily upon themselves. This is illustrated both by the number of sources as well as the particular sources they use for both investment or start-up capital and operating capital. Although this self-reliance is a personal strength, it is also a potential weakness on a macrobasis. Reliance upon only one or two sources of capital, one of which is "self" (whether self-imposed or other-imposed), can serve to thwart the establishment of new businesses or retard the growth of an ongoing business. Hence, it is an issue that deserves close public scrutiny.

## REFERENCES

Albaum, Gerald, Robert A. Peterson, and George Kozmetsky. "Perceptions of Major Problems Facing Small Business Today." *Texas Business Review*, July-August 1983.

Brockhaus, Robert H. "Psychological and Environmental Factors which Distinguish the Successful from the Unsuccessful Entrepreneur: A Longitudinal Study." *Proceedings of the Academy of Management*, 1980.

Brockhaus, Robert H., and Walter Nord. "An Exploration of Factors Affecting the Entrepreneurial Decision: Personal Characteristics vs. Environmental Conditions." *Proceedings of the Academy of Management*, 1979.

Chandran, R., D. DeSalvia, and A. Young. "The Impact of Current Economic Forces on Small Business." *Journal of Small Business Management* 15 (January 1977): 30-36.

Eisemann, Peter, and Victor L. Andrews. "The Financing of Small Business." *Federal Reserve Bank of Atlanta Economic Review* 66 (August 1981): 16-20.

"Financing for Small Business Clients." *CPA Journal* 48 (September 1980): 100-1.

Galbraith, John Kenneth. *American Capitalism*. rev. ed. Boston: Houghton Mifflin, 1956.

Goldman, Robert I. "Look to Receivables and Other Assets to Obtain Working Capital." *Harvard Business Review* 57 (November-December 1979): 206-16.

Gorb, Peter. "Starting Money." *Accountant*, September 21, 1980, pp. 265-67.

Green, L. "Planning and Decision-making in the Small Business." *Managerial Planning*, July-August 1982, pp. 27-32.

Hawkins, Del. *Corporate Policy and Unsolicited New Product Ideas*. University of Oregon, Experimental Center for the Advancement of Invention and Innovation, Eugene, Oregon, 1976.

Jones, Ray G., Jr. "Analyzing Initial and Growth Financing for Small Business." *Management Accounting* 56 (November 1979): 30-38.

Padive, G., and D. Green. "Highlights of the Economic Recovery Tax Act of 1981." *Tax Adviser*, November 1981, pp. 644-59.

Patrick, Thomas. "Employees as a Source of Funds." *Journal of Small Business Management* 18 (October 1980): 55-57.

Peterson, Robert A. *Marketing Research*. Plano, Tex.: Business Publications, 1982.

Peterson, Robert A., George Kozmetsky, and Nancy Ridgway. "Perceived Causes of Small Business Failures: A Research Note." Working paper, the Institute for Constructive Capitalism, University of Texas at Austin, 1983.

Petrof, John V. "Entrepreneurial Profile: A Discriminant Analysis." *Journal of Small Business Management* 18 (1980): 13-17.

Rollins, Henry M. "The Plight of the Successful Small Business." *Texas Business Review* 53 (July-August 1979): 119-24.

Shatto, Gloria M. "The Cost and Availability of Credit and Venture Capital: A Southwest Survey." *Texas Business Review* 55 (January-February 1981): 14-18.

_____ . "Credit and Venture Capital for Small Business Investment." *Texas Business Review* 54 (September-October 1980): 267-71.

Shih, Julie W. "Survey Probes Finances of Small Business." *Economic Leaflets*, vol. 41, College of Business Administration, University of Florida, 1982.

*The State of Small Business: A Report of the President*, Washington, D.C.: U.S. Government Printing Office, 1982.

Swadener, Paul. *A Guide to Venture Capital Funds.* University of Oregon, Experimental Center for the Advancement of Invention and Innovation, Eugene, Oregon, 1976.

Thoryn, M. "Small Business Speaks Out, Government Listens." *Nation's Business*, May 1982.

Tibbits, G. E. "Small Business Management: A Normative Approach." *MSU Business Topics*, Autumn 1979, pp. 5-12.

U.S. Small Business Administration. *The Annual Report on Small Business and Competition: Executive Summary.* Washington, D.C.: SBA, March 1982.

Walker, Ernest, and Leland M. Wooten. "The Two-tiered Economy: Large and Small Business." *Texas Business Review* 54 (July-August 1980): 206-9.

Welsh, J. A., and J. F. White. "A Small Business Is Not a Little Big Business." *Harvard Business Review* 59 (July-August 1981): 18-32.

"What's Going to Happen in '82?" *INC.* Magazine, January 1982, pp. 31-40.

"Where Does Growth Money Come From?" *CPA Journal* 48 (September 1978): 87-91.

Wucinich, William. "How to Finance a Small Business." *Management Accounting* 56 (November 1979): 16-18.

# Part II

# Drivers for Entrepreneurial Activity

## Chapter 3

# Entrepreneurial Characteristics: The Driving Force

## John A. Welsh

Successful entrepreneurship has many aspects. Clearly, there must be an entrepreneur. But there must also be a business concept that has a chance of winning in the marketplace. And the entrepreneur, having that business concept in hand, must have access to the venture capital needed to start the business and support its growth.

Each of these three components – the entrepreneur, a business concept, and access to venture capital – changes with time. The entrepreneur, even one with all the characteristics for success, needs to acquire the experience and skill required to build a business before starting. And later in life there will be constraints on the entrepreneur's freedom to assume the risk of an uncertain income while starting a business. Entrepreneurs travel along a career path on which there is a relatively short segment when the entrepreneur is ripe, so to speak.

Similarly, business concepts bud and bloom, then go to seed. And the entrepreneur's access to venture capital is constrained in time by personal relationships, the condition of the economy, and the regulatory environment of the moment, particularly the rules of the Securities and Exchange Commission (SEC) and the Internal Revenue Service (IRS).

These three components to successful entrepreneurship might be imagined to be the axes of a time-space. The time when each

Excerpted from the book *The Entrepreneur's Master Planning Guide* by John A. Welsh and Jerry F. White ⊚1983 by Prentice-Hall, Inc. Published by Prentice-Hall, Inc., Englewood Cliffs, NJ 07632.

component becomes conducive to the successful creation of a new business might be at the origin of the axes. Then the segment along each axis identifying when each component is conducive to success would represent the edge of a cube in this time-space. This cube might be viewed as a window through which a successful entrepreneurial venture is launched.

The principal component in this portrayal is the entrepreneur — not because the others are of less importance but because somebody has to make it happen. Some person must rise up in that time and place and bring together the many aspects of successful entrepreneurship. The initiating "driver" for entrepreneurship is the entrepreneur.[2]

Entrepreneurs who start glamorous businesses that grow rapidly and become listed on the New York Stock Exchange within five years are clearly outstanding individuals. They are also stand-out individuals. In the setting of the new business, they do not need a name tag to identify them. They are at the hub of the activity, and they are very obviously in charge. Being that outstanding, they must have a set of characteristics that distinguishes them from the general population.

Proprietors of small businesses are like these outstanding individuals, but to a lesser extent. It is easier to recognize these characteristics in the proprietors once you know what you are looking for. With very outstanding entrepreneurs, it is less difficult to identify the characteristics.

The successful entrepreneur whose profile follows is an individual who is clearly the leader in the setting of an entrepreneurial event. The individuals studied to determine these characteristics had each started an ongoing business where none existed before. Each had achieved sales of more than $1 million per year in 1970 (which may be twice that in 1983), each had been in business at least five years, and each's business showed all the signs of an ongoing enterprise that could be expected to continue for at least another five years.

These characteristics do not predict that a person is, or is not, going to be a successful entrepreneur, but they are found to be common among the successful entrepreneurs examined. It would seem reasonable to suggest that a person having these characteristics has a probability of success in proportion to the degree to which they are present.

We have identified 11 characteristics of successful entrepreneurs. These are

1. *Good Health*

Successful entrepreneurs are physically resilient and free of illness. They are able to work for extended periods of time. Entrepreneurs in the throes of building their businesses seem to deny themselves the luxury of illness and will themselves well. Successful entrepreneurs who have suffered chronic health problems, such as hay fever, often report that the symptoms disappeared when they started building their own businesses. It appears that psychosomatic symptoms are also suppressed by concentration on achieving business success.

In a small business where there is no depth of management, the leader must be there. In a starting business there is never sufficient revenue to support the staff needed for all the business functions that must be filled. In lieu of paying others to fill the functions, entrepreneurs fill them with personal effort over extended hours. The work is relentless. The entrepreneur, however, almost never gets sick.

We all know people who utilize at least part of their sick leave each year. We all know people who every year come down with sneezes and sniffles of some sort for three to five days that keep them in bed and out of work. The successful entrepreneurs are not found among this group. Entrepreneurs may have colds and headaches, but they will not allow themselves to admit it. More than that, at the end of the eight-hour day, when their employees return home, the entrepreneur typically continues to work either at the office or at home for nearly another eight hours so that all that must be accomplished for the survival of the business will be completed in time.

We conducted a series of 64 seminars over a four-year period in which distinguished entrepreneurs were asked to tell an audience candidly how they did it. At the conclusion of these sessions each entrepreneur was asked to list, in his or her own words, the characteristics essential to success in an entrepreneurial career. Among the first four characteristics mentioned by every one of these distinguished entrepreneurs was good health.

2. *A Basic Need to Control and Direct*

Entrepreneurs do not function well in traditionally structured organizations. They do not want authority over them. They believe they can do the job better than anyone. They need maximum responsibility and accountability. It is a need for the freedom to initiate the action that they see as necessary. It is not a need for power, especially not a need for power over people. They enjoy creating and executing strategies. They thrive on the process of achieving. Goals achieved are superseded by greater goals. They see the future in their life as within their control, and they strive to exert their influence over future events.

In a large, structured organization, you will recognize these people by their statements, such as, "If they wanted that job done right, they would give it to me and leave me alone." You may also hear them say, "As long as they are running this job, it will never get anywhere." Entrepreneurs behave as if they believe that they are at least as smart as their peers and certainly smarter than their superiors.

This characteristic is primary and dominant in the behavior of entrepreneurs. They have a compelling need to do their own thing in their own way. They need the freedom to choose and to act in accordance with their own perception of what choices and action will result in achievement.

### 3. *Self-Confidence*

Entrepreneurs are fervently self-confident in what they believe possible when they are in control. They tackle problems immediately and directly. So long as they are in control they are persistent in their pursuit of objectives. They are at their best in the face of adversity. Conversely, with loss of control, their involvement and constructive participation diminish.

Entrepreneurs who are starting, building, or running their own business exude self-confidence. Curiously, a small gain in control seems to result in a large increase in self-confidence, while a small loss of control seems to result in an unduly large loss in confidence that a shared objective can be achieved. Entrepreneurs are very self-confident in what they can accomplish when doing it themselves, but they have an uncomfortable feeling working as a team member. Loss of control seems to result in frustration and, sometimes, anger. Greater control seems to result in greater direct action and the appearance of greater self-confidence.

### 4. *Never-Ending Sense of Urgency*

Entrepreneurs seem to have a never-ending need to do something. Inactivity makes them impatient, tense, and uneasy. When in control, and especially when building their enterprises, they seem to thrive on activity and achievement.

Entrepreneurs are not likely to be found sitting on a creek bank fishing unless the fish are biting furiously. They may enjoy fishing, but while in charge and trying to accomplish something, they are more likely to be found getting things done.

Entrepreneurs usually prefer individual sporting activities, such as golf or tennis, over team sports. You may often find them to be downhill skiers. Entrepreneurs prefer a game in which their brawn and brain directly influence the outcome and the pace of activity. They do not seem to enjoy waiting for the rest of the team to pass the ball in their direction.

These people usually have a high energy level. They are frequently characterized as having drive. They have an achievement orientation and a constant, uninterrupted pattern of behavior toward that achievement. They seem tireless in the pursuit of the goals they have set for themselves.

5. *Comprehensive Awareness*

Successful entrepreneurs have a general overview of the entire situation when they plan, make decisions, and work in specific areas. They have a constant awareness of the effect of a single event upon the whole undertaking. They have distant vision and simultaneously an awareness of important specific immediate detail. They are continuously aware of the possibilities and alternatives.

Entrepreneurs maintain their distant vision, but they devote their energy to the step immediately before them. They see the distant mountain, but they concern themselves with the creek in front of them. They are not confused about seeing the forest for the trees.

6. *Realistic*

Entrepreneurs accept things as they are and deal with them that way. They may or may not be idealistic, but they are seldom unrealistic. They want to know the status of things at all times. They want to measure and be measured. News is neither good nor bad so long as it is timely and factual. They seek firsthand, personal verification of data, often bypassing organizational structure. They deal with people the way they deal with functions and things. They say what they mean and assume everyone else does the same. They honor their word. Honesty and integrity flow from this characteristic.

When someone makes a statement, entrepreneurs accept the statement at face value. In the same manner, when entrepreneurs make a statement they assume it will be accepted as stated. During our distinguished entrepreneur seminars, another of the first four characteristics mentioned by each entrepreneur as needed for success was integrity.

This characteristic sometimes gets entrepreneurs in trouble. They are often surprised to find that some of the people they deal with say one thing and actually mean something else. Contrary to the image frequently attributed to them, they are often overly trusting and not sufficiently suspicious in their business dealings.

7. *Superior Conceptual Ability*

Entrepreneurs possess that peculiar raw intellectual ability to quickly identify relationships among functions and things in the midst of complex and confused situations. They identify the problem and begin working on the solution faster than other people around them. They are not troubled by what appears to be ambiguity and uncertainty because they perceive order. They are accepted as leaders because they are usually the first to identify the problem to be overcome. This conceptual ability applies primarily to functions and things; it does not often appear where interpersonal problems need resolution.

Possessing superior conceptual ability is not the same as having a high I.Q. or obtaining higher education. It is an ability to relate functions and things in seemingly complicated and confusing situations. Being realistic, entrepreneurs accept an array of disorganized information and find no discomfort with it. Having a comprehensive awareness enhances this ability.

In the entrepreneurial mode, entrepreneurs seem to be extremely clear in describing their immediate goals and how they will be achieved. If it is pointed out to them that their means to achieve a goal is precluded for some reason, they will almost instantaneously enunciate an alternative means to achieve the same goal with the same precision and confidence they used for the newly abandoned means. Their achievement orientation and their problem-solving ability overwhelm obstacles.

8. *Low Need for Status*

Successful entrepreneurs find satisfaction in symbols of success that are external to themselves. They like the business they have built to be praised, but they are often embarrassed by praise directed toward them as individuals. Their status needs are satisfied by achievements rather than clothes, office decor, or the automobiles they drive. Their egos do not preclude their seeking facts, data, and guidance. They do not hesitate to say, "I don't know," especially in areas outside their own expertise where they are not expected to know.

During the period of struggle for survival and growth, successful entrepreneurs concentrate their resources and energies on essential expenditures for productive assets. They want to be where the action is and do not often find this is an office. It is not unusual to find the entrepreneur's office moved frequently. Likewise, in entrepreneurial enterprises, the organization chart is changed frequently. Entrepreneurs' focus is on the relationship between functions and things and toward achievement. Symbols of achievement and position seem to have little relevance to them.

The significance of these characteristics may be overlooked by casual observers. A business consumes all available assets faster than it can produce them when it is growing rapidly. In starting and building a business, rapid growth is essential to achieve the size needed for stability and equilibrium. During this period of growth the entrepreneur with high status needs will misuse the meager resources available. Successful entrepreneurs find their satisfaction for status needs in the performance of the business, not in the appearance they as individuals present to their peers and the public.

## 9. *Objective Approach to Interpersonal Relationships*

Entrepreneurs are more concerned with people's accomplishments than with their feelings. They generally avoid becoming interpersonally involved. They keep themselves at a distance psychologically. They do not hesitate to sever relationships to help them progress toward established goals. During the period of building the business when resources are scarce, they seldom devote time or assets to satisfying people's feelings beyond what is essential to achieving operational effectiveness and efficiency.

As the business grows and assumes some management structure, entrepreneurs go through a management crisis so predictable that it is classic. Their need for control and its associated relationship to self-confidence make it nearly impossible to divest the authority required by a structured organization. Their strong, realistic approach induces them to seek information directly from its source, bypassing the structured chains of authority and responsibility, and their apparent lack of sensitivity to people's feelings often causes turmoil and turnover in the organization.

Successful entrepreneurs drive themselves and their organizations, think clearly, and are usually mentally ahead of their associates. They are impatient and just do not have the tolerance and empathy necessary for team building interpersonal behavior. They run their own show and delegate very few key decisions. They choose experts rather than friends for associates.

This is not to say that good interpersonal skills are detrimental to the entrepreneur. As the organization grows and there is a greater need for management, the entrepreneur with better interpersonal skills will survive longer as the manager. Most entrepreneurs, however, seem to have only moderate interpersonal skills. Before a new organization has assumed a structure, moderate interpersonal skills are adequate.

### 10. *Sufficient Emotional Stability*

Entrepreneurs have considerable self-control and are able to handle the anxieties and pressures of the business and other problems in life. In stress situations having to do with functions and things, entrepreneurs are cool and effective. They are challenged rather than discouraged by setbacks or failure. But this does not extend to problems involving people's feelings. Entrepreneurs tend to handle these problems by suggesting an action plan. This is seldom perceived as addressing the "feeling" problem.

Entrepreneurs frequently have strong emotional feelings and reactions. They are able, however, to control these at least to the degree necessary to achieve success in their entrepreneurial enterprise.

Where people are concerned, the enterpreneur's superior conceptual ability with functions and things, moderate interpersonal skills, and emotional stability are often inadequate to provide a warm and reasonably stable relationship. On the other hand, contrary to some published reports, the divorce rate among successful entrepreneurs is not higher than that for people in general.

### 11. *Attraction to Challenges, Not Risks*

Entrepreneurs are neither high nor low risk takers. They prefer situations in which they can influence the outcome. They are highly motivated by a challenge in which they perceive the odds to be interesting but not overwhelming. They seldom act until they have assessed the risk. In one sense they may appear to take great risk. They play for high stakes. In entrepreneurland, all personal assets are at stake until the business becomes a very substantial enterprise.

Entrepreneurs are often thought of in terms of the risk they assume. Even the dictionary describes an entrepreneur as one who assumes the risk of business. Like all prudent businesspeople, however, entrepreneurs know that high risking is gambling, not business. They are not gamblers. Entrepreneurs calculate their risks. In fact, they will sometimes appear to be inactive or coasting for extended periods of time. They act only after they have convinced themselves that little, if any, risk remains in the endeavor.

The characteristics found to be dominant in entrepreneurs enable them to succeed at a risk level at which others would fail. They are realistic and persistent. They make sense out of complexity and are confident in the face of adversity. These are traits that carry them on to success where others would be confused and disillusioned and would give up and quit.

Some successful entrepreneurs lack one or more of those characteristics. However, they usually have someone influencing their judgment who is strong in the characteristics in which the entrepreneur is weak. This individual may be a partner or a member of the management team. On occasion this individual is found on the board of directors or among the investors. There are instances when the individual is a mentor, totally divorced from the business, such as a minister, priest, or rabbi. Sometimes this person is a spouse or a relative. There may even be more than one such individual.

There will very likely be competent, experienced production, marketing, administrative, and finance people on the functional management team. They, too, may influence the entrepreneur's management decisions, but these individuals are subordinates on the team. Their advice cannot be perceived by the entrepreneur as decreasing his or her freedom to control and direct the operations. Their role is supportive under the entrepreneur's direction.

There is no scale applied to the intensity of these entrepreneurial characteristics. There is no thermometer on which to say that at 212°F you are an entrepreneur; rather individuals are viewed as having varying degrees of the characteristics.

The characteristics cannot be viewed superficially; although most of us will observe these characteristics in the outstanding entrepreneur, their existence and pervasiveness in any individual cannot be determined by a layperson's examination. To identify the interaction of the characteristics and the extent to which they lie latent at any moment requires an in-depth examination by a trained psychologist with experience and knowledge of these characteristics. That examination would normally take a half day and cost about as much as one good ready-made suit of clothing. The entrepreneur will probably find the experience worth an entire wardrobe.

# REFERENCES

"Are You Entrepreneurial Material?" *Nation's Business* 69 (November 1981): 68.

"Birthplace of Entrepreneurs." *Nation's Business* 69 (December 1981): 18.

Carson, C. R. "How G.E. Grows Entrepreneurs." *Management Review* 71 (February 1982): 29.

Collins, Orvis. *Entrepreneur – Behavioral Study of Independent Entrepreneurs.* New York: Appleton-Century-Croft, 1970.

DeCarle, J. F., and P. R. Lyons. "Toward a Contingency Theory of Entrepreneurship." *Journal of Small Business Management* 18 (July 1980): 37.

Greenfield, S. M., and A. Strickon. "New Paradigm for the Study of Entrepreneurship and Social Change." *Economic Development of Cultural Change* 29 (April 1981): 467.

Gumpert, D. E. "Entrepreneurship: A New Literature Begins." *Harvard Business Review* 60 (March/April 1982): 50.

Hornaday, John A. "Characteristics of Successful Entrepreneurs." *Personal Psychology* 24 (1971).

Kotkin, J. "Entrepreneurial Spirit." *Advertising Age*, sec. 2, March 22, 1982, p. M12.

Lachman, R. "Toward Measurement of Entrepreneurial Tendencies." *Management International Review* 20, no. 2 (1980): 108.

Merwin, J. "Have You Got What It Takes?" *Forbes*, August 3, 1981, p. 60.

Petrof, J. V. "Entrepreneurial Profile: A Discriminant Analysis." *Journal of Business Management* 18 (October 1980): 13.

Rane, P. L. "What Personality Traits Make an Independent Operator Tick?" *Food Service Market* 43 (October 1981): 8.

Smith, S. A. "Psychology of Entrepreneurship: Culture, Motivation and Organization." *Antitrust Law and Economic Review* 13, no. 1 (1981): 45.

Stacey, N. A. H. "Sociology of the Entrepreneur." *Accountant* 183 (November 1980): 851.

Welsch, H. P. "The Information Source Selection Decision: The Role of Entrepreneurial Personality Characteristics." *Journal of Small Business Management* 20 (October 1982): 49.

Williamson, Byron. "A Profile of the Successful Entrepreneur." In *Investing in the Entrepreneur*. Proceedings of the Second Annual Seminar, Staff of the Caruth Institute of Owner-Managed Business, Southern Methodist University, Dallas, Texas, 1974.

## Chapter 4

# Days of Euphoria;
# Moments of Terror

### R. Miller Hicks

When I talk about the characteristics of an entrepreneur, I am really talking about myself. What is he like? What am I like? What spins my motor? I am a pilot, so I would like to paraphrase an expression among pilots. I think an entrepreneur has to balance (and enjoy) days and days of euphoria against moments of just sheer terror! I truly believe that the business is made up that way. It is never clear flying all the way; we always hit some turbulence. But I think it is those tough times, those moments of terror, that really make it fun. They add the spice to an entrepreneur's life. I am not sure I would have as much fun if it was as easy as I would sometimes like to think it should be.

Ingenuity and creativity are essential to an entrepreneur. We should give magnificent awards to a person who has come up with a good business deal or discovered an unusual financial package. In a sense, he is a Rembrandt. Such work is as creative and artistic as anything man ever does, but the entrepreneur does not seem to get the publicity or the public is apathetic.

The entrepreneur has to learn to accept failure. I remember a quote from oil man Sid Richardson when he said, "I have been broke so many times, I thought it was habit forming." Sometimes we think we are omnipotent. That two-edged sword can kill us. It is certainly the toughest thing for me to accept. An entrepreneur must realize that he does not know it all and that he may need a little help.

Concerns about internal organizational factors become especially acute for a small business person when he enters a new venture with a large company. Control Data, for example, is a very good partner of small business because it is acutely aware of small business needs. To help big companies understand small business and to keep the entrepreneurial spirit alive in the boardroom, I would suggest putting an entrepreneur or a small business executive on the board of directors of the biggest companies in the United States.

We are currently going through some reorganization in our own company, R. Miller Hicks and Co. We are now recognizing factors that we had not encountered before marrying a major company. This is the first venture that they have ever engaged in outside of their business, and they have put us through things that I had never even heard of – such as "critical path" and "financial forecasts" with "modes" and "medias." An entrepreneur has to be ready to change internally to meet the demands of the times as well as particular business deals.

An entrepreneur does not need to know the special caveats of every business opportunity, but he had better have a flair for putting the pieces of the puzzle together quickly. For example, I am now producing my first motion picture. I do not know my tail from first base about how to produce a motion picture, but I have two guys who do. I do not have to know how to produce motion pictures. I *do* have to know how to handle the business end of it, how to handle our partner in the deal, and how to get the thing done. (And believe me, if any of you have had experience with the motion picture business, you know that it is one crazy world.)

In flying, pilots talk about "engine-out procedure." What are you going to do when the fan stops turning out there and you are at 8,000 feet? Entrepreneurs play that game in business. I never think I am going to fail on a deal; I am absolutely going to win just like I have it thought out. But I have been around the game long enough that I play a little engine-out procedure with each deal.

What should the role of federal and state government be: laissez-faire, leave me alone, get out of my way! There's an old saying: "If you can't lead, follow; and if you can't follow, get out of the way!" I do not need any help from the federal government. I want them to stay clear of me. (I just wish they would let me keep a few more of my marbles so that I can take another risk every now and then.)

Regional factors can have an important influence on the entrepreneur. Texas provides a special environment for the entrepreneurial spirit. Here you can find the people, the ideas, the talent, and maybe the money to make things happen. From my experience across the country, there is just an altogether different feel here in the great Southwest. In this part of the country, you find fewer people looking for the government handout and fewer entrenched "set-in-concrete" types. We are just worlds apart. It is a fascinating thing for me to see the marked difference in attitude that territory can make.

But we do have a major problem in Texas. I settled in Texas at a beautiful time because there was oil money here. When a guy bought everything he wanted to buy and still had money left over, I would go to him with some crazy business deal, and he would take a flier. This source of money served as a base of risk venture capital for us in Texas. The biggest problem we are facing as entrepreneurs today is the drying up of this risk capital pot. Entrepreneurs need the availability of adequate risk capital. We need a good economic climate, and we need ease of entry. We need to make it easier for young folks coming out of school and for the guys who have been in the company to go into their own businesses.

Small business, through the entrepreneur, provides 55 percent of this country's employment. It creates 86 percent of the new jobs and half the major inventions. The entrepreneur is the future – and probably the only salvation for this country. If I am appreciated for anything as an entrepreneur, I would like it to be as a symbol of free enterprise and as a catalyst who can help turn this country around.

# Chapter 5

# The Role of the Federal Government in Encouraging Small Business

## Alan Chvotkin

One of this nation's great philosophers, Mark Twain, when speaking of the United States, noted:

> We soared into the 20th century on the wings of invention and the winds of change.

His words are again ringing true as we look at this period of time; an explosion of inventions is creating its own winds for change. At the forefront of the development of those "wings of invention" are the small businesses of this nation.

I am the top Democratic staff person for the United States Senate Small Business Committee. The committee is a standing committee in the Congress, with a mandate to "study and survey . . . all problems of American small business enterprise" and report to the Senate our recommendations with respect to those matters.

It is a mandate that we take very seriously. It provides us an opportunity to delve into an incredibly wide range of issues, from general matters like antitrust or tax policy to the specific problems of the service station dealer or the circuit board industry. Through a planned outreach to our constituents — field hearings and occasions for staff to meet and work with entrepreneurs — the committee is able to do a good job of being primary advocates on their behalf in the Senate.

I recently had an opportunity to talk with one of those entrepreneurs who had really made it. I asked if he had any secrets of his success to share. He looked around, took a napkin, and scribbled: "Five easy rules: No money, no education, no brains; buy low, sell high."

I cannot be as concise in my advice, but I would like to focus on the critical, if not pervasive, role of the federal government. With apologies to President John F. Kennedy: Ask not what the government can do *for* you; watch out for what government can do *to* you. Let us go back only a short period of time. One commentator summed up tax policy in Washington in 1981, 1982, and 1983 as: "The government giveth back; the government taketh; and maybe the government taketh more."

In 1981 Congress passed the largest single tax *decrease* in U.S. history. But in 1982 it passed the largest single tax *increase* in history. In March 1983 Congress completed action on the social security reform legislation and — as a means of restoring solvency to those trust funds — accelerated by one year the 1985 planned social security payroll tax increase and moved the 1990 increase up to 1988. In addition, the social security taxes paid by the self-employed were increased. In my view, these tax increases are an additional tax on labor put on business. I wonder whether the impact on employment was given extensive consideration.

In 1982, unemployment rose to a post-World War II high, with almost 11 million Americans out of work. Yet while we in Washington were charged with working on legislation appropriating $4.5 billion "to provide emergency expenditures for neglected urgent needs, to add to the national wealth, and to create productive jobs for women and men rather than make-work," the Dow Jones Industrial had already shattered the magical 1000 mark and is now hovering around record-setting highs of 1160.

While on an issue-by-issue basis Washington policy-making may seem confused, and at times even contradictory, I believe we are united in our desire to create — and foster — an economic, social, and political environment that permits small business to create jobs (which they do in significant numbers) and have a reasonable chance to make a profit. The buck-passing seems to be stopping in Washington.

Policymakers in Washington in particular (but no less aggressively in the states) recognize the critical role of the small business sector in our national, regional, and local economies. The 14 million firms with fewer than 500 employees still employ almost 50 percent of the nongovernment labor force and are the major source of new jobs. They contribute almost 40 percent of the nation's gross national product (GNP).

More and more, I believe, as a matter of economic policy-making, the federal government is recognizing that it ought to target its limited resources to the sectors of the economy most likely to benefit from them. Should not we target assistance to that sector most likely to create new jobs in this country? Should not we target assistance to that sector most likely to create the inventions and innovations in this country? Should not we target assistance to that sector that plays the most important role in providing economic opportunities for minorities and women, both as employees and as entrepreneurs?

I do not have to tell you that this is the small business sector, and we must take these factors into account in the development of our national policies. To a limited extent, I believe we have done so.

As a means of encouraging entrepreneurial development, particularly for small business in the area of high technology, Congress has approved:

- A phased-in, modest set-aside program of federal agencies' R & D budgets to increase small business direct participation in our nation's research efforts;
- Changes in federal patent laws to permit small businesses and universities to retain title to inventions derived in part from federal funds; and
- A 25 percent tax credit for expenditures in R & D (although the Internal Revenue Service's proposed rules are raising significant questions about the availability of this credit for software development).

More than 200 bills have been introduced in Congress between January and April, 1984, to address issues of high technology. These bills focus on issues such as removing restrictions on the innovation process, providing easier access to funds, and ensuring access to quality education and skills training.

The federal government can encourage small business development by eliminating barriers to business entry or growth and by trying to focus efforts in a particular direction through the use of a variety of incentives. In these ways, it has a significant and lasting effect on entrepreneurial activity.

We as a nation have crossed the median from being an industrialized society to being an information-oriented society. While we will always be reliant on our basic industries, our economic *growth* will be determined by the strength and flexibility of our nation's educational system at all levels and by its ability to keep pace with this information explosion.

This year the House of Representatives has already passed the Emergency Math and Science Education and Jobs Act to improve math, science, and foreign language programs (primarily in our nation's secondary schools) and to establish a national policy for training and maintaining an adequate supply of qualified scientific, engineering, and technical personnel. The Senate will consider this and similar legislation shortly.

Legislation will likely be reported again this year to permit a bonus tax benefit to firms donating computers to schools, thereby increasing the "computer literacy" of our students.

Based on agricultural successes over the past hundred years — achieved with the assistance of the land grant colleges from the impetus of federal law (the Morrill Act) — several members of Congress have introduced the High Technology Morrill Act to provide federal assistance for a program of competitive grants to strengthen technological education. The Act is now under legislative review.

There has also been a revived interest in teaching and practicing entrepreneurship in our colleges. The seminal work by Professor Karl Vesper of the University of Washington found well over 200 colleges offering specific courses in entrepreneurship. A recent survey at one eastern university also found that 85 percent of the students were interested in working in a small business at some point in their careers.

We need to keep perspective on the stampede to high technology. Every city in this country will not meet the requirements for another Silicon Valley or Research Triangle Park, but it appears that it will not be from lack of trying.

Although high technology will provide the fastest growth in jobs, it will not be the sector that will provide the greatest number of jobs. In fact, while computer programming may be the most "desirable" job in the coming decade, the U.S. Labor Department projects that the largest number of job openings in the next ten years — as many as 300,000 annually — will be in secretarial work.

It is important, however, to realize that these nontechnology jobs will still require demands for increased education and skilled training far in excess of what we have traditionally considered necessary. The federal government will have a direct influence on the availability of those educational and training opportunities.

It is imperative that we continually remind ourselves of the need to secure our nation's investment in its most precious asset: human capital. It is imperative that we continually remind ourselves of the primary role of the entrepreneur and his capacity for inventiveness in our economy.

Each of these independent variables in the entrepreneurship equation can be seriously and adversely affected by the action — or even inaction — of the federal government.

We who are advocates for entrepreneurs cannot be passive observers. We must be activists on their behalf, encourage them to continually demonstrate their capability, and be watchful of their interests.

The bottom line is that America's business is small business.

## REFERENCES

Fatzinger, G. B. "Federal Small Business Assistance: Review and Preview." *Journal of Small Business Management* 20 (January 1982): 38.

"Go-between for Small Business and EPA." *Chemical Week*, May 5, 1982, p. 18.

Harrison, M. S. "Antitrust, Small Business and the Schumacher Movement: Seeds of a Common Cause." *Antitrust Law & Economics Review* 13, no. 2 (1981): 24.

"Law Moves Money from Large Federal Agencies to Small Business Research and Development." *Industrial Research* 24 (October 1982): 52.

"One-Stop Start-up Aid for Small Businesses." *Christian Science Monitor*, November 19, 1980, p. 9.

Richman, T. "Will the Real Small Businessman Stand Up?" *INC.* Magazine 4 (July 1982): 26.

"SBA's Answer Desk Is at Your Service." *Nation's Business* 70 (December 1982): 15.

"Small High-Tech Firms Seen Reaping Federal Harvest." *Electron News*, November 22, 1982, supp.

"Smaller Businesses and the Tax Act of 1982." *Management Accounting* 64 (November 1982): 16.

Stewart, Milton D. "A New Task for the New Year." *INC.* Magazine 5 (January 1983): 116.

Tanner, R. "High Hopes for 1983." *Venture* 4 (December 1982): 36.

# PANEL DISCUSSION
## ELSPETH ROSTOW, MODERATOR

*Elspeth Rostow:* I pose a question: In the recovery from this particular recession, will the small businessman play a leading role?

We have heard what personality traits characterize the successful entrepreneur: a capacity to take risk; a capacity to get good information and use it effectively; a capacity to manage his or her own affairs; and, above all, the capacity to see opportunities that others have not seen. These are all characteristic American traits because the relationship between high risk and high yield made the economy in the nineteenth century and continues to make it to this day. This is a risky area, but risk and yield are two sides of the same coin.

We also heard the individual accounts of those who have succeeded. Miller Hicks illustrated the importance of regional characteristics of entrepreneurs, and Alan Chvotkin presented a perceptive account of what can and cannot be done at the federal level.

Now let's turn to the impact of the entrepreneur on the economy.

*John Welsh:* Over the last couple of years I have detected certain signs of economic recovery: entrepreneurs are starting high technology businesses and producing jobs and sales well ahead of the general economy in this country. I don't recall seeing that in past decades. Somehow in the last two or three years there seems to be strong entrepreneurial activity destined to lead us out of these present doldrums.

*Alan Chvotkin:* I see the economy, the macroeconomic picture, in a state of transition. We seem to be losing the basic industries, like steel and auto, and the nation's unemployment is stemming in large part from technological change that is creating unemployment that will never be fully regained in those sectors. The early stimulation from the 1981 tax cut (primarily to the individual as a consumer) has triggered recovery. Thus we may have generated an entrepreneurship-led recovery since most entrepreneurs are not corporate legal forms. Of the 14 million small businesses, only 3 or 4 million are corporations; consequently, the primary benefits of the personal tax (the first 10 percent, the second 10 percent, and the coming 10 percent, if it remains in effect) have benefited those entrepreneurs who pay taxes on the personal rate or the partnership rate. They have now found some sources of capital that were previously being transferred to the government. Unfortunately, we still have a deficit and federal borrowing that is too high and draining too much of the gross national product. Unfortunately, I think the recovery that is coming will be slight.

*Miller Hicks*: I have to believe that this economy is going to soar. I don't see anything to stop us unless federal spending gets out of control.

There's another issue pertinent here — the issue of ownership. The problem in big business is that nobody owns it. Who owns General Motors? Nobody. So I don't think you can look to big business to pull us out of this recovery, especially when they're getting their lunch eaten by the Japanese. If you have to pick a segment that is going to lead us out, I submit there isn't a better one than the small business entrepreneurial area. It is our only hope.

But one thing does disturb me. Of 300,000 manufacturers in the United States, only 16 percent export and 84 companies represent the majority of these exports. This is an important area for entrepreneurship. Every billion dollars of export sales creates 40,000 new jobs. We need to help small business become more active in this area, especially through tax benefits.

*Alan Chvotkin*: The role of small business in federal policy has really come of age only in the last five years or so, particularly since preparation began in 1978/79 for the White House Conference on Small Business (which was held in 1980). There has been a Small Business Administration since 1953. But small business as an identifiable sector did not come on the national political scene until about 1977 or 1978. The White House Conference on Small Business came up with 60 recommendations. I just did an analysis of those 60, and over 40 of them have already been enacted into law. That is a very enviable record for any sector.

*Miller Hicks*: A businessman should not be artificially supported whether he's in small business or large. Why in the world should the government come to Chrysler's rescue? They didn't do me, as an entrepreneur, any good about that time. I really can't make the case that you save Chrysler because of employment, labor problems, and so on. I'm in the same boat, though the scale is smaller.

I have my doubts about the political influence of the small business sector. My feeling from Washington is that it sounds good that small business makes up 55 percent of the employment. But my experience tells me that small businessmen are doing the sorriest job in the world. How are you going to get a bunch of independent people together and say, hey, let's have someone up there in Washington represent us? By the nature of the beast, they won't do it; and therefore we don't have the influence in Washington that we should have.

*John Welsh*: Since 1979 some changes in both IRS and SEC rules have had important ramifications. There has been an explosion in new entrepreneurial enterprises; there has been an explosion in venture capital available to back them; and there has been an explosion in the number of venture capital firms looking for investments in this country. I see the decade before us as ripe with new and exciting investments, as rich with new entrepreneurial heroes. How much it will lead us out of recession I cannot say, but we are going to create one hell of a bang.

# Part III

# Entrepreneuring in Mature Companies: The New Technologies

Chapter 6

# The Intrapreneurial Spirit: Taking Risks at Control Data

George F. Troy

The subject of entrepreneurship has always been close to Control Data's heart. The company itself is only 25 years old and still a prototype of the high technology entrepreneurial gamble that paid off. I would like to portray some of the entrepreneurial flavor of Control Data's history, a synopsis of our continuing involvement in and commitment to entrepreneurship, and some thoughts on where we want it to take us.

Peter Drucker once said, "Business has only two basic functions, marketing and innovation." In broadest terms it is innovation that the entrepreneur provides — the idea, the technology, the new process or procedure that offers, on one hand, an increase in real productivity and requires, on the other, a substantial measure of risk. I say "real productivity" because there is no shortage of "paper entrepreneurs" — people capable of tremendous creativity in accounting or finance or legal theory but whose work really involves rearranging existing assets and has no direct contribution to aggregate gain and economic productivity. Also, the extent of the risk taken by a paper entrepreneur usually extends no further than his or her own job, whereas the entrepreneurial activity we are concerned with typically carries with it the potential success or failure of an entire venture. If it succeeds, the real gains will include perhaps the most important of all productivity considerations, job creation.

Entrepreneurship tends to concentrate in individuals and small groups; it arises at least as much from a belief in an idea as from a vision of profits. This was certainly true in Control Data's case.

Back in the 1950s, William Norris was at Sperry-Rand. Along with a small group of associates, he was doing some of the most advanced computer research in the world. He saw the future of data processing and tried to get Sperry-Rand to see it. But they were more interested in their punch card business. So in a pattern that is common to entrepreneurs, Norris walked away from Sperry in 1957 and started his own company. He announced that his company – Control Data – was going to design and build supercomputers. Keep in mind that during the 1950s some "experts" had studied the emerging technology and decided that six big computers could handle the whole world's computing needs for all time. In terms of technology and risk, then, the birth of Control Data was a classic new venture.

In the early years the company rode the entrepreneurial roller coaster. Every few years the company had to gamble everything on its newest computers. In the space of ten years, the price of Control Data stock went from $1 a share to $140 and then back down to less than $20. There was wild growth followed by recessionary droughts followed by more wild growth. At one point the company cut everyone's pay to stay afloat – although it never cut back on research and development. There were the "go-go" years of the 1960s when Wall Street discovered high technology. But there was also brutal competition. Even some of the biggest names eventually failed in the computer business, companies such as RCA, Bendix, and General Electric.

Under Norris, Control Data succeeded through a continuing process of innovation and risk taking. Two crucial and controversial decisions involved expanding into Office Equipment Manufacturers (OEM) computer peripherals manufacture and then into data processing services. In both cases there was substantial opposition within the company, in addition to the usual outside skepticism. But these and other all-or-nothing entrepreneurial decisions turned out to be the keys to Control Data's transition from a very vulnerable start-up technology firm into what is today a secure Fortune 200 company.

We now have sales in excess of $4 billion, and our business interests include a great deal more than computers. But we are young enough and lucky enough to still have with us many of the company pioneers, including, of course, Bill Norris. As a result the entrepreneurial spirit has always been highly prized and promoted within the company, even to the point where some analysts complain that we are constantly moving away from our bread-and-butter businesses into risky and unusual projects.

You may have seen the *Wall Street Journal* article several months ago. "Far Out Firm," the headline said, "Seeking to Aid Society, Control Data Takes on Many Novel Ventures." Well, it is true. But it is no more than the realization that we got where we are through innovation and that any success we have in the future, especially in the competitive technological field, will be the result of more innovation. And true innovation is the distillation of entrepreneurial activity.

Almost from the beginning, Control Data spawned other businesses. Bill Norris has often said that if someone has the entrepreneurial drive, he will never be happy until he has exercised it. So the company had for many years an informal policy of encouraging and assisting people who wanted to go out on their own. Probably the best example is Seymour Cray who designed many of Control Data's early computers. With Control Data's help, he went on to found Cray Research and began producing the Cray computers.

We realized two things out of Seymour Cray's leaving. First, because some good people are always going to move on, there ought to be a mechanism to make the most of it for both Control Data and the employee. This led eventually to our Employee Entrepreneurial Assistance Office, which I will discuss. Our second realization was that by providing an environment that was conducive to innovation in the first place, Control Data was able to reap the benefits of Cray's technical brilliance for as long as we did. The important thing is that innovation occurs, and Norris's position has always been to accept whatever risk that requires.

About 12 years ago, Control Data began to formalize a policy that had been developing for some time, and it is now our fundamental corporate strategy. It is to envision society's unmet needs as profitable business opportunities. What this means is that instead of simply making a product and then trying to market it, we look at needs that already exist and try to tailor business solutions to satisfy them. It is an entrepreneurial strategy. First comes the idea, and if it is good enough, the profits will follow.

Of course, there is no shortage of things we need as a society, from cheaper energy and improved health care to a stronger farm economy and more available and affordable quality education. Control Data has projects under way in each of these areas and dozens of others. Our Plato system of computer-based education, for example, has been in development for more than 20 years, and we expect it to be our biggest revenue source in the not-too-distant future. We have businesses in urban revitalization, farming in Alaska, technology transfer overseas, and vocational training for data processing professionals. Somewhere in the "novel ventures," as the *Wall Street Journal* calls them, are the future businesses of Control Data. By applying a social need strategy, we are virtually certain to be targeting huge and permanent markets. So the question of how successful we are depends on execution and innovation – in other words, our own entrepreneurial abilities.

One of the most pressing needs we are addressing is job creation. It is no secret that the majority of new jobs and entrepreneurial innovations come from small business. Yet small businesses, particularly in the technology fields, are at a tremendous competitive disadvantage. Acquiring critical and affordable expertise, technology, equipment, facilities, and a hundred other things a big company takes for granted is often impossible for a start-up company. As a consequence most start-ups fail, taking jobs down with them. At the same time, almost all the resources these businesses require do exist in large companies, where they are often underutilized.

Several years ago Control Data concluded that we could realize additional income from our own past investments by making available to smaller companies our underused or dated technology, along with professional and management expertise and support services. One expression of this is the creation of business and technology centers. These are physical plants that provide various combinations of consulting services, laboratories, manufacturing, and office space as well as other services that facilitate the start-up and growth of small businesses. Economies of scale make it possible to provide business and technology center tenants and small companies nearby with needed facilities and services of higher quality at considerably lower cost than they could get elsewhere.

Nine business and technology centers are now in operation and more are being established. The concept is already yielding significant results. For example, the national failure rate for small businesses is roughly 80 percent after five years. At the oldest business and technology center in St. Paul, Minnesota, this failure rate has been cut to 14 percent after three years. Although this is not a direct comparison, the trend is unmistakable.

Control Data is also assisting small business by promoting public and private cooperation across a broad front. One effort is the Minnesota Cooperation Office (MCO). The MCO's approach is simple. An entrepreneur has an idea for a new product or service and wants to start a company. He or she comes to the MCO, and MCO helps develop a business plan and obtain financing. The permanent staff of the MCO is small, but a volunteer advisory panel of engineers, scientists, and executives evaluate and assist in preparation of the business plans. Because the plans are expertly conceived, the chances of receiving financing and achieving economic viability are increased accordingly.

In addition, Control Data is active in the Minnesota Seed Capital Fund and the Help Start a Company Program, both of which do what their names suggest.

Another major business thrust is my organization, Control Data Business Advisors. Our senior management recognized that smaller companies had a need for experienced professional assistance. Major consulting firms typically have no interest in these companies, and the resources they do have access to — local accounting firms, for example — are by nature rather limited. At the same time, the expertise required by these companies did exist within Control Data. So Business Advisors was formed to identify that expertise and market it. The company was set up with key Control Data employees, and we were given access to the rest of the 50,000 Control Data people around the country as a talent pool from which to draw resources.

We were also given the ability to cannibalize Control Data's internal operations for anything we felt could be sold externally. Right away we found a series of things like occupational analysis and employee attitude surveys that, with some very simple repackaging, amounted to more than $1 million in revenue in my organization last year. We are doing this same thing in the financial area and with technology.

Control Data has any number of technologies that — by the company's standards — are outdated but that still have a market and a use. Business Advisors will be in a position of identifying these and selling them to smaller firms throughout the country.

Business Advisors and these other efforts serve a number of purposes. They further Control Data's business strategy by addressing the need for job creation through a healthy small business sector. They also provide potentially lucrative markets for Control Data's goods and services. Finally, they offer a way for Control Data itself to flex its entrepreneurial muscle. Take Business Advisors, for example. As established Control Data executives, we have been put out in a new business and charged with making it profitable. No amount of "paper entrepreneurship" is going to help us. We must deliver results. Similar satellite Control Data businesses are under way in dozens of areas.

There is a deep commitment within the company to promote entrepreneurship at every level, inside and out. It is part of the culture that has grown with the company, and it is also based on the knowledge that in a high technology business when you lose your creativity, you have lost your company.

Control Data has always had a policy of encouraging employees who felt they had to break off on their own. As long as we were going to lose them anyway, we believed we may as well do it in a positive way. So three years ago we formalized the policy into an Employee Entrepreneurial Assistance Office. This is a confidential service that gives employees a place to go to test out their ideas and get help exploring the possibilities. If their concept is sound, the office will help in writing a business plan and obtaining financing. Since the program started, almost 600 employees have been helped, and 61 new businesses have been started – everything from an antique shop to a magnetic disk refurbishing shop. The key figure here is that 330 new jobs were created.

Even though the policy is successful, it still concerns us that a lot of good and creative people are being lost and with them a lot of good business opportunities. In effect, we are helping them leave rather than trying to get the benefit of their entrepreneurship within the corporate framework. In the case of a person who wants to open an Italian shoe store, it is not a concept that fits Control Data's strategy. But what about the Seymour Crays? For those people and those ideas there ought to be a structured way for the company to both foster the entrepreneurship and receive some of the benefits. This is the area we are working in now, and our approach is a form of what has become known as *intrapreneurship*.

Unlike the entrepreneur who starts up a venture on his or her own, the intrapreneur would develop an idea with the full support of the company. The corporation, in fact, would do much the same for the entrepreneur as the venture capitalist. But the intrapreneur would develop a new business *within* the corporation to the mutual benefit of both.

The basic issue that intrapreneurship addresses is, Do employees really have to leave their corporate positions in order to achieve their goals? Must an organization squeeze out individuals with new ideas instead of creating an environment for them to develop those ideas into thriving new businesses?

From the employee's point of view, the advantages of intrapreneurship are obvious. They take a limited risk regarding their individual economic situations. They can utilize the know-how of the corporation. They can use machinery and tools during slack times for design and testing. They have access to the marketing organization, given some special rules. And they are entitled to, and expected to, look upon the environment with a different perspective. They are endowed with special means to develop new business that the corporation might otherwise have overlooked or started to develop much later. On the other hand, their special status must be reciprocated through some sort of guarantee to the corporation that its interest will be enhanced by the intrapreneur's activity. To this end, some general rules seem to apply:

1. The business should be consistent with, but not identical to, the company's own goals.
2. The company should take an equity position in the new business, thus participating in both the risk and the reward.
3. The individual should take a well-defined risk – for example, a 10 percent salary reduction that would apply toward his or her own equity position.
4. The intrapreneur should have a well-defined reward based on the development of the business.
5. Since the business is to be independent, there should be rules facilitating buildup of capital.

Along with these rules, the concept suggests a variety of questions and problems. How many employee intrapreneurs can the company work with, and how does it choose? What about people with high expectations who cannot be accommodated? How do you structure the benefits of the intrapreneur, and how much should the company invest in a given project? What support would a corporation give in terms of flexible scheduling, in-kind services, and relief from other responsibilities? What about the line managers who have worked long, hard, and loyally for the company for years who now see a bunch of new people getting corporate support to go out and get rich on their own? Clearly, there are questions to be answered about intrapreneurship. But just as clearly, the answers are worth pursuing, and Control Data is in the process of doing so.

Let me now jump ahead to where Control Data's policies on entrepreneurship are likely to lead. In addition to all the things I have mentioned, a logical next step will be to begin spinning off existing functions from within the company, particularly the staff and service functions. In any large corporation the big expenses are personnel, administration, and real estate — the corporate General and Administrative (G & A). Suppose for a minute you could spin these off and use them only on an as-needed basis. There would be no benefits expense, no facilities expense, and no salaries. Instead, the corporation would utilize a roster of closely aligned independent contractors, with all the advantages that brings, such as responsiveness, competitive pricing, and so on.

At a deeper level, there is the advantage of a stabilized work force. The company keeps a central core of key employees and functions. In good times, we contract work out and use supplemental employees and temporaries, always keeping a certain percentage of our goods and services coming from outside vendors. Then, in the recessionary times when cuts must be made, the core employees are protected.

There is a flip side to this. If Control Data were to spin off a number of functions — taking an equity position or negotiating a beneficial contract beforehand, just as with the intrapreneurs — and if things go sour, we do not have all our eggs in one basket. We have pieces of companies (dozens, even hundreds) in every kind of business and discipline. In effect, we become a holding company for a network of smaller companies that we have fostered and that could conceivably grow up and begin to spin off the next generation of businesses.

All of this is in its earliest stages. But it is a workable plan, and Control Data is in a good position to accomplish it. Our history and our business strategy point toward it; above all, we have kept the entrepreneurial commitment to pull it off. In the end, it may be more of a risk not to try it.

## REFERENCES

Adkins, L. "Creating a Climate for Productivity." *Duns Business Monthly*, vol. 199, May 1982.

"Control Data Beats the Industry." *Business Week*, November 30, 1981.

"Corporate Executive Office Formed by Control Data." *Electronic News*, July 15, 1980.

Naditch, M. P. "Wellness Program Reaps Healthy Benefits for Sponsoring Employer." *Risk Management*, vol. 28, October 1981.

Norris, W. C. "Computer-based Education in New Areas and Partnership in Productivity." *Computers & People*, vol. 30, May-June 1981.

_____ . "Developing Corporate Policies for Innovation: A Program of Action." *Long Range Planning*, vol. 14, August 1981.

Rohmann, L. "Get 'Em While They're Young." *Forbes*, August 2, 1982.

"A Social Strategy Aimed at Profits." *Business Week*, June 25, 1979.

"Thinking Big: That's How Control Data Has Spurred Its Growth with Computers." *Barrons*, December 14, 1981.

"William Norris, Chairman & Chief Executive Officer, Control Data Corp." *Industry Week*, October 27, 1980.

# Chapter 7

# Applying Technology to Demands: Expanding Markets at MCI

## Charles M. Skibo

MCI is one of today's high growth companies and as such is founded on the twin pillars of robustness and entrepreneurial spirit. Vital to both is our view of marketplace opportunities and our assessment of technology, their effects on our efficiency, and how they will help us grow.

At the outset we should define the industry in which MCI competes. In 1982 the market was about $45 billion and is expected to grow to $63 billion by 1985 (Figure 7-1). Some 91 percent of this $63 billion market consists of three long-distance services:

- Private Lines — constituting 9 percent — are mostly used by large corporate business or government; these are dedicated circuits end to end;
- WATS (Wide Area Transmission Service) makes up 15 percent and is typically used by medium to large businesses; and
- MTS is direct distance dialing, and it is the largest segment at 67 percent; in this service, customers are sharing a network on a dial-up basis.

The remaining 9 percent of the market is made up of international voice and data, domestic data, and paging and cellular telephone services.

In order to serve this huge and expanding marketplace, MCI has changed its corporate structure to include three operating subsidiaries (Figure 7-2):

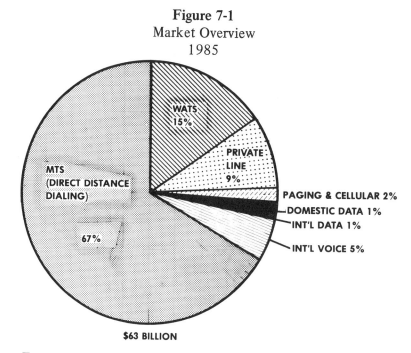

**Figure 7-1**
Market Overview
1985

$63 BILLION

⊠ WATS  ▢ PRIVATE LINE  ▢ PAGING & CELLULAR  ▣ DOMESTIC DATA
▣ INT'L DATA  ▢ INT'L VOICE  ▨ MTS

*Source*: Constructed by the author.

- MCI Telecommunications will concentrate on our domestic telecommunications business; last fiscal year's revenues were $920 million;
- MCI International is our international operating company, which had revenues of approximately $127 million; and
- MCI Airsignal will provide paging and mobile phone services, including cellular radio.

MCI's goals in the short term are twofold. First, we plan to continue doing what we do best: buying sophisticated technology and selling it to a customer base. Second, we buy, operate, and merchandise technology to provide telecommunications services in growth markets.

MCI offers four basic long-distance telephone services (Figure 7-3). Through MCI Telecommunications, our domestic long-distance

**Figure 7-2**
MCI Corporate Structure

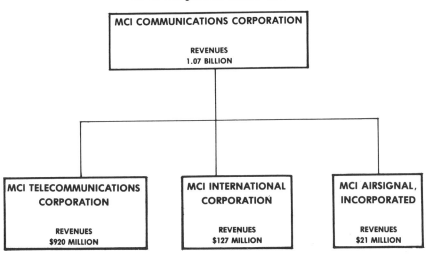

Source: Constructed by the author.

**Figure 7-3**
MCI Telecommunications
Revenue by Service

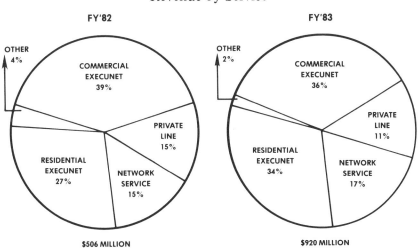

Source: Constructed by the author.

telephone, we provide Execunet service to direct distance dial customers, both business and residential. These individuals or businesses, who pay a $10 per month subscription fee for unrestricted access or $5 for limited access, dial into our network and share its capacity on a demand basis. We also provide Private Lines, and our network service competes with Bell's Wide Area Telephone Service, or WATS. Residential Execunet was the fastest-growing market this past year and now constitutes 34 percent of our total revenue. We entered this market in March 1980.

Customer growth and use of our system since 1981 has been explosive (Figure 7-4). In 1981 we had a customer base of 100,000. In March 1983, two years later, we had 1.3 million customers. In two more years we expect our customer base to grow to 3.8 million customers.

**Figure 7-4**
MCI Customer Base Growth
Fiscal Years 1981 to 1985

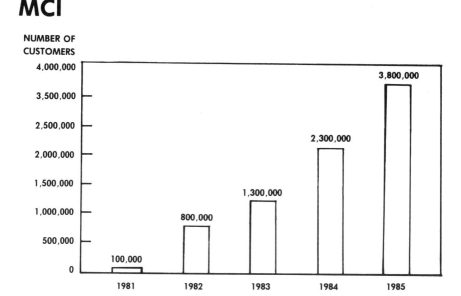

*Source*: Constructed by the author.

Our first objective, then, is to take what we do best and apply it in expanding marketplaces. Second, we intend to become a telecommunications services company capable of providing customers a full range of offerings that will suit their communicating requirements. These services will be designed for economy, convenience, and efficiency.

With the acquisition of Western Union International (WUI) last June, we expect to participate in a large way in the growing domestic message market. It is our plan to handle the domestic segment of international message and data traffic on our own network. WUI's ability to secure international traffic from domestic customers is no longer confined to business delivered to WUI by Western Union Telegraph at one of the five so-called gateway cities. WUI may now go into the United States at large to secure customers. Their use of our network to do so will not only cut their costs but also provide ready access to most of the country's major metro areas.

International voice communications to and from the United States has until recently been a monopoly of AT&T. From the standpoint of U.S. policy, this market dominance no longer is protected. We plan to enter this market as soon as we can work out operating arrangements with the foreign public telephone and telegraph administrations.

The WUI acquisition also provides MCI with a springboard into the paging and mobile radio market through WUI's subsidiary, Air Signal. The mobile radio or cellular telephone market has dynamic growth potential, and it has the same technical and market characteristics as our present business. To date, we have filed with the Federal Communications Commission (FCC) for authority to serve the nation's top markets for cellular telephone service.

As with cellular telephone service markets, the same can be said of the data, record, and message markets. These today constitute a relatively modest share of our traffic. But their growth is obvious. And our commitment to serve them parallels their rise. Last July the FCC approved our applications to offer digital termination service in some 40 major cities. This concept envisions the end-to-end transmission of data. In providing this service we will use many of our existing facilities, supplemented by those engineered strictly for data traffic.

The growth of our business continues to be paced by our ability to construct and put in service new plant and facilities. In the last

three fiscal years we have significantly increased our plant investment (Figure 7-5). Last year we spent over $725 million for new
equipment, sites, and construction. This brought our total physical
plant investment to $1.48 billion at fiscal year end. We expect to
invest a little over $1 billion in the system this year. This means
that at the end of this fiscal year a full 70 percent of our technology
will be less than 24 months old.

What will be some of the impacts of new technology? Currently,
MCI's microwave routes typically carry 14,700 channels of capacity.
During the next year, we plan to install digital radios along some of
our routes that will increase the capacity to over 29,000 channels. We
have a development project under way with two vendors to provide
single sideband radios utilizing analog — the net effect will be the
addition of another 23,000 channels. Thus over the next two years,
we will have the ability to expand our existing high traffic routes
to over 52,000 channels. These new technologies are more cost
effective than existing ones. In addition, we can utilize existing right-
of-way paths and existing towers with minimum of modification.

**Figure 7-5**
MCI Capital Investment History
(FY 1980-84)

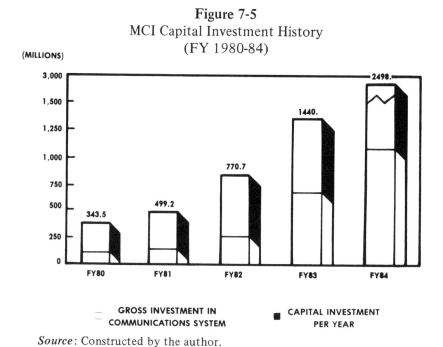

*Source*: Constructed by the author.

By avoiding new route construction, we can save the company a considerable amount of money.

MCI has a significant amount of work under way in building fiber optic routes around the country. This mode of transmission will be commonplace in the next three to five years. Our first route between New York and Washington will be complete by December. This will add 40,000 circuits of capacity, which can be quickly expanded to 120,000 circuits. Today our microwave route between New York and Washington has less than 12,000 circuits. We will also build routes between Washington and Chicago, and from Chicago to Dallas and Houston.

MCI is also positioning itself for an enormous opportunity ahead as a result of the Bell companies divestiture. When this occurs, starting in September 1984, the Bell companies will be required to give us the same type access that they give AT&T Long Lines. In effect this will open 50 percent more of the market to MCI (rotary dial telephone market). It will mean that our customers will not have to dial extra digits to use our system. Most important, every Bell customer will be given the right to choose whom they want as a primary carrier. Today they automatically choose AT&T, but we believe that given a free choice many will select MCI.

To service this burgeoning demand, we have acquired 24 transponders on two satellites that will be launched in the next 18 months. This will add 75,000 circuits of capacity to our system. To put this in perspective, we have a total of 60,000 channels in our network today.

Increasing efficiency in the use of our plant is important. A measure of efficiency of a capital-intensive business is the amount of revenue we can produce for each dollar we invest in the plant (Figure 7-6). Each dollar of average plant investment produced 85¢ in fiscal year 1982 compared with 56¢ the year before — a 52 percent improvement in efficiency. In fiscal year 1983 and 1984 we are holding constant because of the inordinate amount of up-front investment required to position ourselves for future opportunities related to divestiture. Nevertheless, as a reference, our information indicates AT&T Long Lines produced 47¢ in revenue per dollar of average plant investment in 1982. We are about two times more efficient in use of plant than our major competitor.

Another measure of productivity we use is the annual revenue generated per employee (Figure 7-7). We increased our revenue per employee from $183,000 in fiscal year 1982 to $208,000 in fiscal year 1983. As a reference point, we estimate that AT&T's Long Lines revenue per employee in 1982 was $96,000. That means that we are about twice as productive in the use of people.

The entrepreneurial character of MCI is reflected in our corporate culture and organization:

*   MCI is decentralized; we put heavy responsibility and authority at the lowest level;
*   The company is aggressive and opportunistic when it comes to exploiting technology for the marketplace;
*   We are a customer oriented, market-driven company;
*   We have an attitude of "can do" and "get it done today"; and
*   We are young, very entrepreneurial, and risk taking by nature.

There is a great deal of opportunity at MCI. We have been historically expanding our employment base by about 40 percent per year. We expect to continue this pace over the foreseeable future.

**Figure 7-6**
MCI Telecommunications
Revenue per $1 Capital Investment

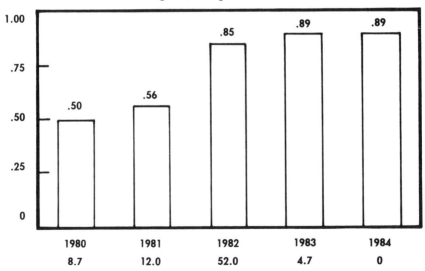

% INCREASE FROM PREVIOUS YEAR

*Source*: Constructed by the author.

**Figure 7-7**
MCI Telecommunications
Average Revenue/Employee
5 Years

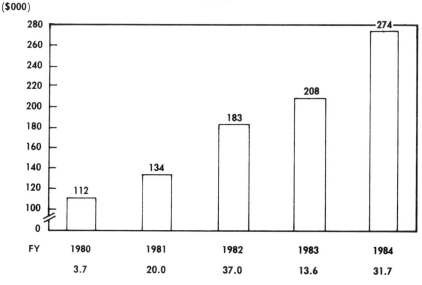

Source: Constructed by the author.

The past few years have been highly successful ones. The company is determined to become a full-service, one-stop shopping center, if you will, for telecommunications services. The markets we plan to serve are enlarging, and the opportunities for growth are increasing. We believe our goals position us well as the telecommunications industry undergoes major changes.

## REFERENCES

"Funding Fast Growth at MCI." *Business Week*, October 5, 1981.
Gay, V. "AT&T Competitor MCI: Long Distance Long Shot." *Market & Media Decisions*, vol. 17, April 1982.
"Getting Stronger All the Time." *Financial World*, May 1, 1982.
Levy, R. "Dreamer at MCI Communications." *Duns Business Monthly*, vol. 199, March 1982.

"MCI Builds a Long-Distance Future." *Sales & Market Management*, January 18, 1982.

"MCI Buys WUI for $185 Million." *Broadcasting*, December 21, 1981.

"MCI Official Outlines Competitive Future." *Telephony*, April 5, 1982.

"MCI Provides Many Services to Match Customer's Needs." *Telephony*, October 12, 1981.

## Chapter 8

# Streamlining Operations: The Vertically Organized Unit at IBM

### Robert Moeser

International Business Machines (IBM) is in a very competitive business. Consequently, it is essential that we behave in an entrepreneurial manner. To understand this corporate orientation, it is important to consider the goals that IBM has set for the 1980s and to see how these goals relate to the type of activities that I shall describe.

There is a twofold perspective on this entrepreneurial nature. First, my view is that of a professional manager — one who is perhaps somewhat of a pragmatist and one who has been out of school for a number of years. Second, we cannot forget that IBM is a $34 billion corporation.

One goal that IBM has set for the 1980s is to expand our traditional business and in the process develop new entrepreneurial activities. To maintain our competitive edge, we must not only strengthen our position in current markets, but also look to opportunities in emerging markets.

A second goal is to stay in the forefront of technology. This means that we must emphasize quality. And by that I include the reliability, the accessibility, and the serviceability of our products as they are perceived by our customers. *Quality* at IBM is all-inclusive. It is not just the quality of the product or the statistical control techniques that are associated with the quality control "function." The term refers to the essential nature of everything that is done in the organization. It is my fundamental belief, and that of our corporation, that this is the quintessential piece of the fabric that is IBM and the central core of our strategy. For example, passing defect-free work through our indirect structures will not only eliminate cost and expense, but it will also contribute to superior excellence in everything we do.

A third goal is to stay in the forefront of value. This means that we must give our customers what they want and at the same time remain the low cost producer, the low cost seller, and the low cost administrator. To achieve these goals, we have to be entrepreneurial.

We feel that we now have the strongest competitive product line in our history. We have small systems growth, and we are moving into the world of office automation, which continues to be a very successful area because we have applied some new ways of doing business. For example, we now have product centers where we do retail marketing. We also do IBM direct telemarketing. In addition, we have established independent business units within the corporation, one of which I will describe.

The personal computer is an example of an independent business unit that is set up within the corporate infrastructure. It has a mini board of directors, which sets policy for that unit. It is really a company within the company. Consequently, it does not have to go through many of the corporate approvals that are usually required in large corporations. Instead, it has many powers that were formerly reserved for the corporation and that are now reserved for the board of directors. Hence it can move very rapidly. It can capitalize itself — it has access to capital. It is essentially a streamlined small business operation that is more competitive, more innovative, and thus truly entrepreneurial in style and substance.

One might ask, Why does not IBM do this for the whole corporation? We have other major product lines involved in information systems that are integrated tightly among our numerous facilities. Because they require massive interdependencies, it is not possible to establish independent business units for them. Therefore, the company must be selective in finding those areas that will benefit by such a style.

To appreciate fully the need to do things differently and to be an entrepreneur in a large company, you have to look at the nature of competition. Competition drives what an organization is really trying to do. You have to look to the bottom line and ask, What are you optimizing on? Clearly we must optimize on product cost because we compete in an extremely competitive area. To deal with low cost competitors, a company must act entrepreneurially and may thus have to change its approach.

A low cost competitor provides products in high volume. There are few models and very few features on them. The processes that manufacture these are vertically integrated to a high degree. There is maximum utilization of capital. This does not mean they are of necessity highly capitalized, but it does mean that assets are highly leveraged. As you leverage your capital assets with very high volumes, there must be few changes in these processes to ensure high stability. As a result manufacturing cost priorities are critical. Because of the contemporary importance of manufacturing, the low cost competitors have a high manufacturing cost priority. So, they have frozen schedules that are easy to deal with, and long-term supplier commitments are vital. This arrangement allows the company, once again, to leverage its inventory assets by turning them faster, and it gives a better rate of return on controllable assets. This all implies simple logistics — which translates into less cost. This is the nature of the competition. In addition, there is unique manpower utilization, which calls for simple operations, little movement, and high non-regular content.

The material content of products among low cost competitors is roughly the same, but the differences are in the overhead. So how do you compete, given that kind of situation with those leverages? Entrepreneurial skills must be applied at the product level. How? One way, as we did with the personal computer, is to bring a product into the marketplace quickly by unencumbering it from the normal corporate structure.

To unencumber a product from the corporate structure, the unit should be organized vertically. By that I mean you identify a leader and give that person the opportunity to deal with all required functions. I purposely refer to *leaders* as opposed to *managers* in this instance because the people who get involved in these efforts must have a capacity to lead others.

Once a leader is identified and given authority, he can deal with four key functions: cost engineering, production facilities, production control, and quality control. He can then identify what is an allowable cost in his product. Quite literally, that leader can then see, for example, how many secretaries he can afford in his product cost. Once that vertically organized unit is partitioned off from the organization, it can really begin to work.

A large organization tends to optimize functionally. In a manufacturing organization, for example, you would tend to find the assembly operation optimizing on its needs, the production control operation optimizing on its needs, and so on. The sum total of the optimization, however, is not really where the firm wants to go. Instead, somebody with entrepreneurial instincts must be given the authority to make the trade-offs and to optimize where the company really wants to be optimized — at the bottom line, the cost level. That person must be allowed to find the leverages to compete. This is a significant and subtle development that occurs when a large company breaks these kinds of organizational units off and allows them to operate more entrepreneurially.

A small company atmosphere can now be juxtaposed with the inherent support structures that exist in a large company. This is an advantage in a large corporation that does not exist in a small corporation. The results not only reduce the risk of the venture but also contribute to developing a common spirit. By applying these kinds of entrepreneurial techniques, a large company can, in addition to the other benefits, build cohesive teamwork into a project. The end product is highly focused objectives that can be managed and met.

## REFERENCES

Bertig, R. T. "IBM's Strategy for the Office." *Computer Decisions*, April 1982.

Charon, K. P., and J. D. Schlumpf. "IBM's Common Staffing System: How to Measure Productivity of the Indirect Workforce." *Management Review*, vol. 70, August 1981.

Heier, S. "IBM's Science of Simplification." *Institutional Investor*, vol. 14, November 1980.

"IBM Enterprise Concept Addresses Major Challenge." *Infosystems*, vol. 27, November 1980.

"IBM Takes Automated Route to Better Productivity." *Traffic Management*, vol. 21, November 1982.

"IBM: The Giant Puts It All Together." *Duns Business Monthly*, vol. 120, December 1982.

"In The News: More Commotion Coming: IBM's Aggressiveness, Says Its New Chief, Has Only Begun." *Fortune*, March 9, 1981.

Verity, J. W. "I(BM), Robot." *Datamation*, vol. 28, April 1982.

Wallace, R. "IBM Details Plans for Lab of Future Market." *Electronic News*, June 21, 1982.

# PANEL DISCUSSION
## ROBERT F. LANZILOTTI, MODERATOR

*Robert Lanzilotti*: Today we are witnessing what the late Joseph Schumpeter talked about. The process of creative destruction has visited a devastating blow to corporate America. The initial reaction, as I view it, by U.S. corporations and by government was to sound the alarm for the reindustrialization of the United States. This was useful only insofar as it focused the attention of important people on the critical problem. But this focus was badly misplaced because the attempt to recapture industrialization was misplaced. We need to gear up for the postindustrial economy. We have to reharness the entrepreneurial spirit, the visionary mind, that is associated with the innovative character of our country's economy.

There has been a response from the business community. I hope that this response does not follow the reindustrialization theme, because it is neither possible nor desirable to regain a past that is forever gone. Business firms across this country, especially big businesses, are engaged in major search to find their corporate souls. Governments and universities have been enlisted to aid this rather bewildering and agonizing question — to recast, to regain, to recapture the animating principles of our major corporations.

Our charge is to explore the viability and the sustainability of the entrepreneurial spirit in all size corporations, especially the large ones. The question is, Can mature companies nurture and retain the innovator? In defense of big business — and I think some defense is in order — I note that some of our major corporations, as represented by Control Data, MCI, and IBM, have attempted to avoid the stultifying effects of bigness and bureaucracy by the use of subsidiaries, smaller units, self-contained projects, and more individual delegation of authority.

Let's consider some specific issues. First, one clear example of emerging technology is cellular telephones, requiring both major resources and entrepreneurial spirit.

*Charles Skibo*: Cellular telephones are mobile telephones that one would use typically in an automobile. Today, however, there is usually only one transmitter or receiver radio beaming out in a city; because of this restriction, the market is small. Cellular telephones break the city up into very small cells, with each cell having a transmitter and a receiver. There is a single computer centrally located that directs your call and automatically puts you over into the next cell as you go from cell to cell. This provides two or three advantages. It provides a tremendous amount of capacity for serving the marketplace and therefore drives the cost way down. In three to five years, it will be commonplace to have a phone in your car. You will probably also have a phone on your watch.

*Robert Lanzilotti*: AT&T Long Lines have access to the same technology that you have. How do you plan to continue, over time, to undercut them on cost?

*Charles Skibo*: Let me give you an example. AT&T built a fiberoptic system from Boston to Washington, and they are taking it on to Richmond. They used a state of technology that we think is inappropriate, and we think ours is about 30 percent more efficient. They put the first one in. We came in about a year later and used the latest state of technology.

In addition, AT&T has an awful lot of plant built up because they thought they were a monopoly. They found out differently. They do have a monopoly on the long-distance segment, but not much longer. (The local operating companies have a monopoly.) When you have a monopoly, you often have a tendency to overbuild and overstaff. That is why we are about two times more cost effective in utilizing people than they are.

To more specifically answer your question, we are working with a lot of vendors who have all the same kinds of capabilities – and probably more motivation – that AT&T does.

*Robert Lanzilotti*: The telecommunications development is interesting in that it triggered a dramatic change in government policy. There is no doubt that the policy shift was prompted by MCI's activities and has thus revolutionized telecommunications.

Recently, the government has been involved with IBM on some very high speed integrated circuit programs. What direction will such programs take in utilizing this technology in industry?

*Robert Moeser*: I am not specifically aware of those programs, but let me comment on how we operate and perhaps peripherally get at the intent of the question. We do an enormous amount of research and development involving many areas, including large-scale integration. The bulk of that flows into our products at one point in time or another — if it is a business opportunity and can be made profitable. It is just that fundamental. Any of the work that we are doing now we will put into products when economically feasible. In our development laboratories, people who are called *systems managers* are responsible for the selection of the technologies that are going to be used in their products. This decision is made at quite a low level in the organization.

*Robert Lanzilotti*: How are we going to get technology to the marketplace from a competitive point of view?

*George Troy*: One interesting way is a joint venture started by Control Data called MCC — Microelectronics and Computer Technology Corporation. There are 12 companies involved, including Control Data, Advanced Micro Devices (AMD), Honeywell, and Motorola. Their specific purpose is to do research and development and to take it to the point where a firm can bring it to market. Then it is marketed through the individual companies. Why have competitors combined forces? In high tech it is the only way to compete.

*Robert Lanzilotti*: Control Data seems to have realized that some employees are going to leave the company, so you may as well try to help them become successful. Can you share with us a short example of an employee who went to the center for help and how he or she actually got started?

*George Troy*: We had a refurbishing operation for some of our hard disks. More and more, we saw that we really did not have a need for that particular activity. There were a couple of employees who were involved and decided that there was a business for it. They went to the employee entrepreneurial office and laid out what they considered to be a business plan. Control Data management, through the employee entrepreneurial office, looked at that business plan, made the decision to let those employees purchase that operation, and set it up in a way that provided a long-term buy out. Control Data had no equity in that company. It is 100 percent owned by the employees. This is essentially how the process works.

The program is a vehicle for the employee. When he first comes to the entrepreneurial office, he doesn't have to tell his supervisor. As a matter of fact, we suggest that he not do so because he or she may not want to go into business after it is all done. The office points out the hardships they may encounter as well as the benefits they have with Control Data. If they decide that they still want to do it, then the company takes the position: "Well, why not?"

*Robert Lanzilotti*: Is there something at the top of mature, large corporations that attenuates risk taking? I am wondering if there is a casualty of entrepreneurship as we move the innovative minds and idea men into the chief executive officer spots. As they become administrators, do they lose the spirit to encourage what they themselves fostered? Does the organization have a tendency to kill the entrepreneurial spirit as it gets larger and more bureaucratic?

*George Troy*: I will speak with a bias. Bill Norris is still probably the greatest entrepreneur in Control Data.

*Robert Lanzilotti*: Is that the exception that proves the point or is the Norris example characteristic of the genre?

*George Troy*: I don't think he is characteristic. This gets back to the point about leaders — there are leaders and there are managers. As we get involved in a new business, the leader is usually the person who starts it. He gets the innovation in there; he gets the risk takers in there. Over a period of time, usually about three years, his skills are no longer as appropriate to that operation; so we bring in what we call a *manager*. He goes in and cleans up the mess — because entrepreneurs always leave a mess.

*Charles Skibo*: Bill MacGowan is our chairman, and he came in during the late 1960s. Bill is an entrepreneur, but he is fundamentally an outstanding businessman. That is why he has been able to continue to control the corporation while still being very entrepreneurial and keeping the company that way. The people who are heading our three subsidiaries are not only entrepreneurs but also good businessmen. These are the people we put in charge.

*George Troy*: Corporations are not necessarily looking for the entrepreneur to be the chief executive officer. But the cream rises to the top; success breeds success. In many cases the entrepreneurial type who moves into that type of position, by the nature of the beast, isn't going to be able to run out in two weeks and start up a new company and then run off again. Maintaining the attitude of looking ahead — and not getting caught up in the next quarterly report but maintaining a vision of the future — is the part of the entrepreneurial spirit that is the most important thing for a large company to keep in mind.

## Part IV

# Entrepreneuring in Emerging Companies: The New Technologies

## Chapter 9

# Flexibility and Stability in a Growing Company

Harry Keirns

The entrepreneurial spirit is one of the real backbones of this country. We must preserve it and foster it.

The company in which I am a principal, KMW Systems, is relatively small and truly entrepreneurial. We do about $4 million in sales right now, although we expect to grow to $8 million next year. We have 43 people and we are six years old. Our strategy has been to maintain total control of the company through its formative years, even though not going outside for capital has slowed our growth. We determined to really concentrate on long-term goals rather than on immediate returns on the assets employed.

Basically, we consider ourselves in the business of problem solving. Our tools are programming techniques and highly integrated digital electronic circuits, usually a single chip. Our products are in a relatively narrow area that fit tightly together. Our initial products were in hard copy graphics. Hard copy graphics involve creating a permanent image on paper film as opposed to a temporary image that you might create with a cathode-ray tube. We chose computer graphics because it was an area we knew about, and it was an emerging technology, and an exploding market.

Graphics has had a great impact on companies designing complex products, such as automobiles and airplanes. It has been able to greatly reduce the time required to design these products and thus to lessen their cost. It is now being used increasingly in the business world. The old adage that "a picture is worth a thousand words" can be clearly understood when you look at a trend chart for a company's stock prices for a year. You can readily see what is happening. (Try looking at a piece of paper with 365 numbers — it is not easy to visualize what that stock is doing.)

Later, we added products to our graphics line that enabled us to communicate with computers both locally and remotely. It was necessary to do a systems job for the companies with which we were working. Soon we were approached by other companies that said, "We would love to communicate with these computers. Can you build your product for us?" So all of a sudden a communications product was born for us. This has led to two divisions, again closely tied together, because much of our systems sales are in both areas.

I think the ability to recognize the difference between an opportunity taking you in a positive direction toward your overall goal as opposed to an opportunity taking you in a diversionary direction away from it is the key to getting a company going right. It is not always an easy thing to see where opportunities will take you. But if you have a clear understanding of what your goals are, it becomes less ambiguous.

Corporate executives like to talk about in-depth planning and credit themselves with a lot. But, in truth, luck probably has much to do with business success. In everyone's life, and especially in an entrepreneur's, you get some good and some bad luck. You try to keep the bad luck from killing you while trying to capitalize on the good. In fact, to constantly evaluate opportunities in light of the rapid changes a young company goes through is really one of the most exciting things an entrepreneur does.

Early in our life, KMW Systems was very undercapitalized because of our choice of going on our own, growing from profitability, and borrowing what we could from banks. Consequently, we were willing to take on special projects that had some sure profit attached to them. But now if someone asks us for a special job, unless it is really consonant with what we wish to do, we put a high price tag on it. We must strive to maintain clear corporate focus.

Entrepreneurial characteristics are something I can certainly relate to. Thomas Edison once said that his formula for success was 99 percent perspiration and 1 percent inspiration. I concur with that. The most important thing I look for in partners on the management team (and I have been in a couple of start-ups now) is an absolute commitment to do whatever is necessary to get the job done, to meet the goals. I am willing to sacrifice anything but my ethics to get the company moving. I would rate creativity and intelligence next, then experience, and finally pragmatism. You have to be pragmatic when you are in a small company struggling for life and growth.

In a small company, when the management team shares mutual goals, it does not take much time to evolve decisions. The time consumed is largely for implementation.

Not having rigid rules is sometimes a blessing. The management team that runs our company has had experience working for corporate giants. We learned some good management techniques, but we also saw some to avoid at all cost. We consciously try to perpetuate the environment of a small company — one with small project teams, where everyone participates in the goals of the corporation.

Everyone in our company, down to the person on the manufacturing floor, has a feeling that he is part of the firm's success. We tend to be paternalistic: we grant stock to the people in the corporation; we have a profit-sharing plan; and we have semiannual dinners where we review our financial performance and cover everything from current budget to future plans. This approach has produced benefits. We have a zero turnover in people; few people are absent from work; and it is not unusual to come in at night to find people there working, developing ideas and getting excited about them.

There is another blessing in not having rigid rules: we have more flexibility in rewards, challenges, and especially the people we pick. Two of our most valued employees illustrate what I mean. We hired a fellow who was a Xerox technician. He repaired Xerox machines. He tried to get into their engineering area for years, but he had no degree. When we met him, he talked to us about a job and enthusiastically told us about his hobby at home. He had built a computer out of parts and interfaces. His whole house was literally filled with computer toys. We turned him loose. Here is a person with much native intelligence who for whatever reasons never had a formal education. He was just hitting a power curve, where he really wanted to do something, when we brought him in. He is now one of our lead engineers. The other employee is a fellow who was a managing director of Aramco. We picked him up after Aramco forced him to retire when he reached 62. Because he is vibrant and has tremendous abilities, retirement was driving him crazy. We hired him, and he has proved to be a great asset.

We are currently examining the wisdom of bringing in outside capital because with additional monies we can increase our growth rate. Even if someone had given us substantial money several years ago, it would have been difficult for us to have grown faster than we did because our own abilities as leaders were somewhat limited.

We are looking at a number of possibilities. We are considering a public offering. One of the things that dismays us is how much a good public offering will cost us; in our estimate, about $250,000 for auditing fees, printing costs, and legal fees alone. Then 7 to 10 percent of the offering will go to the underwriter. We are looking at potentially $500,000 to $1 million worth of additional capital and thus have to seek $3.5 million or $4 million to even make the offerings attractive. So we may end up selling out a healthy chunk of the company for a minor amount of need. As a result the idea is again on the back burner.

Another reasonably attractive approach is to work with a venture capital company. One of the advantages here is that we could get, at the same time, some good advice — because these people certainly would be both experienced and committed. On the negative side, venture capitalists usually pay less than the public markets.

Finally, we are looking for a private investor. We would like to find someone wealthy enough to qualify under the blue sky laws so that we do not have to do all the registration and filing under Securities and Exchange Commission laws. This may even get us someone who is very astute and can be added to the board to provide some direction. As my partner likes to put it, "You pay your money and you take your choice." What we may also do is go back to the bank for debt financing for another year.

The ability to attract capital investors can be critical to a new start-up, especially if it is capital intensive. Our business segment was not especially capital intensive. We were able to develop our early products by using board-level computer products integrated with original ideas. Slowly, as our production became higher, we abandoned board-level products, designed our own, and started to reduce costs — thereby improving our margins. Consequently, we were ready to face the inevitable increase in competition.

There are many companies that go into areas where capital is needed much earlier in the cycle. They may have to grow faster to compete in an established market. For instance, right now our protocol market in communications has gone from zero to $15 million in three years. We are now starting to attract heavy competition. One of the reasons we need to grow faster is because we feel that in order to be successful we have to keep a strong market share. With only a small share of the market, a company may not be able to compete. This is why it is vital, no matter what your strategy, to be able to get capital when circumstances warrant it.

One of the issues we had to confront when we first started the company was where to locate it. We started the company in Cleveland, Ohio, but felt it was probably going to be difficult to attract many good people there. So we all threw names in a hat and came up with 21 cities for possible locations. We structured a large matrix in which the cities labeled the rows and all of the relevant factors labeled the columns. Our final matrix stressed suppliers, quality of living, cost of living, availability of native labor, transportation, financial institutions, and educational facilities, in that order. We filtered the list down from 21 to 3 cities. We visited these cities and chose Austin. How much our Austin location has contributed to our success is a subjective determination, but we feel it has certainly been a key element. It has not only been easy to attract people to this area of the country, but Austin has also been growing as an electronics center. We are happy with the choice.

The interests of the United States as well as those of entrepreneurs — who are the key to our country's success — can be best served by the government's providing good ground for fledgling industries. In this context, government must provide as much stability as possible. The importance of stability is reflected in something that happened to us early on. We took a contract to manage a corporation that was involved in real time resource allocation. They worked with police and fire dispatch via computers, so that when a call came in, the client would be quickly able to get the right force to meet the emergency. Because a new technology was involved, this company had been aggressive about marketing its product. It was willing to take rather slim profit margins to get the technology into use. Although the company was initially going along very well, it was dealing with the kind of project in which almost all of the monies were at the end. There were few progress payments, so the small company was debt financing the project all the way along. Then the prime rate soared eight points. Suddenly, marginal profit ratios became very negative. The company is still alive, but it had to scale back its activities. This is sad, considering its high promise. It is an example of what macroeconomic instability does.

I recently asked someone who represents us in Israel, "How in the world do you ever live in an economy where you have inflation rates of 80 to 100 percent a year?" He said, "Well, it's not really very difficult. As long as you are stable, you can plan for it. What really kills you is when you plan for one thing, but the situation drastically changes. Then it is just impossible to do business."

All things considered, I highly recommend the life of an entrepreneur for those who want to build things. In spite of all the problems, the challenges and the rewards are tremendous.

## Chapter 10

# The Evolving
# Business of Life

### Robert M. Nerem

In considering opportunities for entrepreneurship, it is appropriate to stress technologies where we have an edge on the rest of the world. One such area is what I call *the evolving business of life*. Of course, for a long time there has been a substantial biological business — for example, biological compounds, chemicals, and pharmaceuticals. However, there is now emerging both a biomedical engineering industry and a biotechnology industry.

Let us consider the following headlines that have appeared over the past year in local newspapers and news magazines:

"Living on Borrowed Time — Barney Clark Gets the First Permanent Artificial Heart";

"Mighty Mice — Gene Transfers Create Giants";

"Making the Body Transparent";

"America's $39 Billion Heart Business";

"The Hoechst Department at Mass General."

The author thanks V. L. Hollyer for her assistance in the preparation of this chapter.

We as a public are continually being bombarded with headlines like these. What was once an imagined industry is undergoing a fast transition to big business, with all the attendant challenges and opportunities as well as problems. In order to better understand this evolving industry whose business is life, let us consider some of the segments and some of the specifics.

## MEASURING THE BODY'S VITAL SIGNS

One important segment of the biomedical engineering industry is that concerned with measuring the body's vital signs, that is, measuring everything a physician always wanted to know (and some things he did not). Over 15 years ago, when I first began to work in the area of biomedical engineering, there were hundreds of companies, all small, seldom employing more than a few dozen professionals, and many, if not most, having a single product line. This cottage industry made everything from blood pressure measurement devices to instruments for measuring heart rate and blood chemistry to a multitude of other "black boxes" designed to measure physiological variables. It was an industry in which a young engineer seeking a job had considerable difficulty finding an initial position. These were not the kinds of companies to interview through campus placement offices. Rather, these companies might only hire one to two engineers a year, and they relied solely on personal contacts and letters of application. A graduating student literally had to write hundreds of letters in order to have a good chance for a position.

One such example is Millar Instruments, Inc., in Houston, Texas. It was founded in 1971 in the garage of Huntly Millar. This company had a single product line: catheter pressure transducers. Although the company is branching out into other areas, initially its market was cardiovascular pressure measurements, and the product was largely sold to basic and clinical researchers wishing to make accurate measurements of the arterial pressure time history.

The company has grown over the past 12 years and now has 45 employees. This year its gross revenues will be more than $1.5 million. Furthermore, over the last decade it has become increasingly clear that the conventionally used fluid-filled catheter produces a pressure output that may have a considerable amount of artifact. This not only concerns basic and clinical research, but it is also important in patient diagnosis (the little "wiggles" really do mean something). Thus Millar Instruments expects to expand its business considerably through sales to clinicians, not only for cardiovascular measurements but also in the areas of urological and gastroenterological measurements.

## IMPLANTOLOGY

One segment that has grown significantly over the last ten years involves products that are implanted in the body. These include everything from artificial hips and knee joints to cardiac pacemakers and artificial heart valves to less known devices such as intraocular lenses. Although we are far from being able to produce the "bionic man," people are being helped in ways we could not have imagined 20 years ago.

A major company in this area is Intermedics, Inc. (their motto is Our Business Is Life), which was founded in 1973 as a supplier of implantable cardiac pacing systems. Since its inception, this company has become one of the world's fastest growing biomedical engineering companies. This growth has taken place through an expansion of its cardiac pacing business as well as through diversification into other product areas. The company achieved a successful human implant of its first cardiac pacing product – a mercury-zinc pulse generator – in 1974. Since then, it has introduced the lithium-powered pulse generator, a transtelephonic monitoring service (1975), the first multiprogrammable pacemakers (1978), and a new generation of pacemakers with advanced space-age telemetry features (1981).

The diversification of the company began in 1976 with Intermedics Intraocular, Inc., and in 1978 Carbomedics, Inc., was added. In 1979 it became affiliated with ZyMOS, a manufacturer of custom integrated circuits, and in 1980 a joint venture was announced for the development of implantable infusion devices for the controlled delivery of medications. In 1981 both Intermedics Orthopedics, Inc., and Calcitec, Inc., were formed, the former to manufacture reconstructive orthopedic prostheses and the latter for the development of calcium phosphate-based compounds for orthopedic and dental applications. Over the last five years the company's revenues have increased to over $200 million, and although its net earnings fell in 1982 (primarily owing to problems in the pacemaker business), this company has enjoyed extraordinary success.

## MAKING THE BODY TRANSPARENT

In 1905 Wilhelm Roentgen, in discovering the X ray, opened the first window into the living body and inaugurated a new age in medicine. As significant as this was, the basic X-ray system has its limitations. Although bone structure is well-defined, the picture gives little sense of depth and many of the softer tissues of the body are but fuzzy gray shadows. Thus the picture is one purely of anatomy, and even in that sense the limitations are severe.

Ten years ago a new kind of X-ray machine was introduced. It uses a computer to construct clear, cross-sectional views of the body. The CAT scanner (computerized axial tomography) revolutionized radiology, providing a way to carry out noninvasive diagnostics, compelling virtually every large hospital in the country to invest in one of these $1 million machines.

The introduction of ultrasound to diagnostic medicine has also been an important breakthrough. With ultrasound one sees anatomy from the echo or the reflection of the ultrasonic waves; one can also measure flow by using the principle of Doppler frequency shift. Ultrasonic devices of various types are in wide use, particularly in cardiology departments.

There are two newer concepts, however, that appear to have the potential of again revolutionizing the business of noninvasive diagnostics. One of these is positron emission tomography (PET) and the other is nuclear magnetic resonance (NMR). While neither of these imaging systems has the resolution of the CAT scanner, they do offer the possibility of being able to noninvasively measure parameters associated with the chemistry of the body.

PET involves the use of radioisotopes that emit two 511 kilovolt photons after the interaction of a positron with an electron. The positrons are emitted from the isotope; when a positron encounters an electron, which is negatively charged, there is an annihilation, leaving two high-energy photons that fly off at 180° from one another and that can be detected by an array of scintillation crystal phototubes in timed coincidence. The PET technique has potential for the measurement of sugars, fatty acids, amino acids, and other metabolic substrate as well as receptor concentrations anywhere in the body.

PET is a valuable research tool for the investigation of life processes, especially in difficult-to-study diseases such as aging, schizophrenia, atherosclerosis and heart disease, and cancer. Although work is proceeding on instrumentation, radiopharmaceuticals, and modeling, the real need is for biological information as a prelude to clinical usage. Although PET involves small risks from the ionizing radiation, as in other diagnostic procedures the benefits should far outweigh these dangers.

The development of the PET technique is limited by the fact that the radioisotopes required have a short half-life and thus must come from an on-site cyclotron facility. A cyclotron is most popularly thought to be an "atom smasher." However, it is a major facility both in size and in terms of financial investment. So there are only a few PET facilities in the country. One of these is under development at the University of Texas Medical School at Houston where the Division of Cardiology will be applying the PET technique to study and diagnose cardiovascular disease. A cyclotron has been under construction, and although the company providing the cyclotron has gone bankrupt, it is expected that the cyclotron in Houston will become operational soon. The other major item required for PET is a camera, that is, the scintillation crystals and phototubes required to detect the colinear photons. Such a camera is also being constructed at the University of Texas Medical School. The application of the PET technique can be divorced from having an on-site cyclotron facility, and as the cost of a camera comes down, it should then be possible to provide clinical PET diagnostics to patients at a reasonable cost.

Nuclear magnetic resonance is another possible image for your future. The basic requirement for an NMR device is a large magnet and a radio frequency coil. When placed within an NMR field, the nuclei of hydrogen, phosphorus, and other elements align themselves with the field. A high frequency pulse is then generated that creates a second field at right angles to the first. The molecules align themselves to this second field. When this radio frequency pulse is turned off, they return to their original position, producing a detectable electromagnetic signal through the process. Each type of tissue in the body has a characteristic signal intensity and duration. When this is fed into a computer, the data create a cross-sectional image of the body. Although it has been said that NMR opens up the whole world of in vivo chemistry, in fact its primary application is in detecting water density and certain phosphate compounds. However, it is viewed as being able to improve greatly our ability to diagnose conditions associated with the brain.

The FONAR Corporation has been at the forefront of the development of NMR imaging. Back in the early 1970s, Ray Demadian was using NMR for spectroscopy studies. He conceived of an idea for applying NMR to making images and proceeded to develop the technique along these lines. Initially he sought funding from the National Cancer Institute and the American Cancer Society. However, having absolutely no success there, he set up a private, non-profit foundation to seek out funds, and he used these to support the development of NMR imaging in his laboratory. In 1975 the group he had organized began thinking in terms of a corporate structure, and a private offering was made in June 1978. This was extended in 1981 with a small public offering. The FONAR Corporation now has an NMR imaging unit that is on the market and that operates with a resistive magnet. The future for this type of imaging, though, appears to lie with superconducting magnets.

Another company that is heavily involved in the diagnostics business is Diasonics, Inc. Diasonics was formed as a limited partnership in 1977. In February 1983 they had one of the largest initial public offerings ever made when $122.9 million was raised. Diasonics's technology is ultrasound, digital X-ray computer imaging, and NMR. Other companies involved in making NMR imaging systems are General Electric, Picker International, and Brooker, which recently had one of their NMR units installed at the Baylor College of Medicine in Houston.

## SHAPING LIFE – AND A BUSINESS – IN THE LABORATORY

Gene splicing is a technique vital for progress in biological research. Though simple in concept, it is complex in practice. The basic objective of recombinant DNA (deoxyribonucleic acid) techniques is to insert a foreign gene for a desired product into an organism under conditions such that the characteristics of the foreign gene will be expressed more abundantly than those of the native genes. This approach has generated many of the recent advances in cell biology.

Lewis Thomas stated, "It seems only yesterday that cell biology was the purest and most basic of all fields in biomedical research, in constant need of defense before skeptical congressional sub-committees, hard to justify for taxpayers' funds on grounds of rather vague prospects for its future usefulness, years off." He went on to say, "Now, almost overnight it looks like a way to make lots of money."[1] Now nearly 200 genetically based companies have been founded by scientists/entrepreneurs. At the head are five com-panies: Biogen, S. A.; Bethesda Research Labs; Cetus; Genentech; and Genex. Even for these five, their greatest attribute is the promise that lies ahead. There is little doubt that by the year 2000 this will be one of the largest industries in the country.

Genentech, Inc., is generally considered to be the leader. It is a south San Francisco firm founded in 1976 by venture capitalist Robert Swanson and University of California biochemist Herbert Boyer. This firm has pioneered in the creation of about a dozen protein products by recombinant DNA techniques. The company has a staff of more than 350 of whom approximately 70 have Ph.Ds. Their budget for research and development is $20 million per year. Although this budget is small in comparison with some of the larger companies in this country, Genentech has a record for creating major new projects that no other company in the pharmaceutical business has matched in recent years. During the third quarter of 1982, its human insulin product became the first human health care product of a recombinant DNA technology to reach the market. Approval of this new insulin came just five months after Food and Drug Administration (FDA) authorization was sought and only four years after Genentech scientists, working together with the City of Hope National Medical Center, had produced the first human insulin in the laboratory. This new insulin is being manufactured and marketed under the trademark Humulin by Eli Lilly and Company, pursuant to a licensing agreement with Genentech.

## THE FLOW OF IDEAS

The fact that Genentech brought its human insulin to the com-mercial marketplace only four years after it was first produced in the laboratory points out one of the major problems for the bio-technology/genetic engineering industry and even for the biomedical industry. The products being marketed are only a short timestep away from the basic research laboratory. This is true for genetic engineering, and it is equally true in such areas as PET and NMR imaging. One of the basic questions that a company in such a rapidly escalating area must address is how to keep the flow of ideas coming that will generate the products needed just a few years hence.

For Genentech, this is being done by having the best features of an academic environment, including a minimum of micromanagement, the encouragement of journal publications, and excellent research facilities. Furthermore, scientists there have been given equity positions in the company. In high technology companies, top scientists may well need to be tied to the company through arrangements where top business management is contractually hand-cuffed to the firm. Furthermore, although it seems only yesterday that the academic research laboratory was viewed as an ivory tower, it is clear that for the high technology companies of tomorrow the academic environment, which has been so successful in spawning new scientific ideas, must be captured in spirit by the company and/or the company must develop specific linkages with universities.

The most striking example of the latter is Hoechst AG, a German pharmaceutical firm that has founded (some would say "bought") a molecular biology department at Massachusetts General Hospital in Boston. This new department will have a staff of 50 with ample research facilities, and its senior scientists will be recommended for faculty appointments at Harvard Medical School with which Massachusetts General Hospital is affiliated. Hoechst's contractual guarantee over the next ten years is approximately $70 million. However, this is a minimum contribution and could well be supplemented if the research effort is productive in ways that are valuable to the company. In exchange for the $70 million plus, Hoechst receives exclusive worldwide rights to any patentable licenses that emerge from the company-sponsored research.

This is not the only example of academic-industrial linkage. E. I. du Pont de Nemours & Company will spend $6 million over five years to support a new genetics department at Harvard Medical School. Rockefeller University has a five-year, $4 million contract from the Monsanto Company. Washington University in St. Louis also has a large contract from Monsanto. And there are others. In all of these the contractual issues are the same. Is the funding to be exclusive of other support? And what is the agreement with regard to patents, licenses, and royalties? What is the institution's obligation to the company in terms of conducting designated scientific programs, sending reports, and training company personnel? Will the scientific personnel have faculty status? If so, what other duties are allowable? Will the scientists have the right to publish and to collaborate with others? These are not easy questions.

Beyond the immediate impact of a particular agreement between a profit-making company and an academic institution, there are broader issues of public policy involved. For example, will the binding of a specific university laboratory to a specific company reduce communication between colleagues (some say there is already a change in atmosphere around the biology department coffeepot)? Will research priorities be distorted by the focus on the development of marketable products? Will the content and direction of student educational programs be likewise influenced by profit motives? These questions are important, not just to a particular institution but to the nation if we are to maintain technological leadership.

In spite of these inherent problems, this whole area needs to be addressed seriously. In some sense, universities have become too dependent on federal research support, and if a better balance can be achieved between federal and industrial support of basic research, this would not be all bad. As part of this, Congress and governmental research agencies need to consider how the United States can best foster industry/university linkages for the future.

## BUT IT TAKES MORE THAN GOOD SCIENCE

As important as the flow of ideas is to the success of a company operating in the high technology arena, good science and good engineering are not enough. Companies driven by science and technology appear to have had a higher-than-average failure rate. It is likely that of the nearly 200 scientist/entrepreneur-run companies that have been formed recently as part of the biotechnology industrial surge, over one half will either fail or be taken over by larger, presumably better-managed firms.

As one example of the uncoupling between science and business, there is no country that has enjoyed better science, at least in terms of quality if not quantity, than Great Britain. Cambridge and Oxford represent the epitome of academic excellence, and such recent break-throughs as CAT scanning, NMR, and the unraveling of DNA have roots in British research and development. However, as admired as their science is, Britain is not equally admired for its industrial leadership.

In a recent article Sir Charles Carter, past president of the British Association for the Advancement of Science, attempted to analyze this seeming inconsistency. He noted that "the successful use of science depends on the quality of management, from which derives the attitudes of the firm and the quality of its various actions." Carter goes on to argue that senior management must have a suffi-ciently sympathetic understanding of the areas of science relevant to the work of the company to be able to make sensible judgments on what the experts recommend to them. This does not automati-cally imply, however, that senior management should themselves be qualified scientists (although there is no reason why they should not be either), for senior management also needs to be equally sympathetic in their understanding of marketing, production engi-neering, systems planning, finance, personnel relations, and so on. Furthermore, Carter points out that it is a mistake to suppose that you get "a balanced policy by linking together a set of narrow and blinkered experts in the areas of the firm's actions." What is needed, he argues, is that "integrating personality who possesses breadth."[2]

An example of a single-minded outlook is a company (not to be named) that not too long ago raised $8 million in venture capital to develop a vaccine against malaria. This company is driven by first-class scientists of the type who would be considered a plus in an evaluation by any venture capitalist and who will most likely be successful in developing the vaccine. However, they are not giving adequate attention to such seemingly obvious questions as: Who actually will buy it? How will it be delivered? And who will do the vaccinating? Undoubtedly, there are equally tragic examples of companies that are single-mindedly driven by accountants and/or lawyers. One of the real challenges for any high technology company is how to blend, how to integrate, the science with the business.

Beyond questions of fostering scientific creativity and inte-grating technology and management, there are other problems that should not be overlooked. Two of these are regulatory risks and pro-duct liability. With regard to the former, the FDA is a major factor not only for pharmaceuticals (and this includes those genetically engineered) but also for virtually all medical devices. The term *product liability* needs little further elaboration. There is no question but that there will be interesting liability questions raised if, for example, a consumer is poisoned by a food that uses genetically manufactured substances. There will also be increasing international competition that will mandate the continued flow of ideas if we are to maintain our competitive advantage in world markets.

In his recent article Sir Charles Carter said, "There is no doubt of the capacity of science to produce further marvels, but there is doubt about the capacity of human beings to use wisely and well the opportunities provided."[3] The biomedical engineering/biotechnology industry is ripe for continued development. It is a prime area for the entrepreneurs of the 1980s and 1990s. In spite of hesitations and even setbacks over the short term, the science is there − this is an area where we have an edge on the rest of the world. Investors are there. Furthermore, the rising cost of health care mandates a solution. Whether technology is part of that solution, and whether this business of life continues to evolve as an entrepreneurial industry, depends on whether we have the human capacity "to use wisely and well" − and I would add *successfully* − the opportunity that now presents itself. This is the challenge.

## NOTES

1.  L. Thomas, "Notes of a Biology Watcher: On Science Business," *New England Journal of Medicine* 302 (1980): 157-58.
2.  C. Carter, "Conditions for the Successful Use of Science," *Science*, March 18, 1983, pp. 1295-98.
3.  Ibid.

## REFERENCES

"Agribusiness Genetic Engineering − $50+ Billion Annually By 1996?" *Food Processing*, vol. 42, July 1981.
"Biomedical Market Projected to Reach $20 Billion by 2000." *Chemical Market Report*, November 8, 1982.
"Biotechnology Becomes a Gold Rush." *Economist*, June 13, 1981.
"Biotechnology's Ties to Academia Assessed." *Chemical Engineering News*, April 26, 1982.

"Government Boost for the Biotechnology Industry." *Business Week*, December
    14, 1981, p. 110.
"Great Biotech Gamble." *Management Today*, October 1982, p. 59.
Lyman, F. "New Life Forms for Fun and Profit." *Business and Social Review*
    40 (Winter 1981/82): 40.
Nash, E. "Full of Promise — But All in the Future." *Advertising Age*, September
    27, 1982.
Nossiter, D. D. "Designer Genes: Biotechnology Is Big in Promise and Pitfalls
    for Investors." *Barrons*, February 22, 1982, p. 8.
Stagen, G. J. "Soft-Cell Approach to Biotech Stocks." *Barrons*, February 22,
    1982.

## Chapter 11

# The Role of the Venture Capitalist in the Entrepreneurial Process

## Lucien Ruby

In 1972 I decided to start a company, and I managed to convince some very foolish venture capitalists to put up $750,000. Not a bad amount for 1972! But being from a traditional Southern family that was entrepreneurially oriented, I had to do one thing. I had to go back to Kentucky and talk it over with the patriarch of the family, my Uncle Hooks, who was about 90 years old and had never been in good health. When I got there, Uncle Hooks was in the hospital. He had tubes running in and out, and there were monitors going every which way. I walked in, pulled up a chair right beside him, leaned over, and outlined the deal in his ear. He did not open his eyes. He lay there until I finished the description of what I was going to do. I even gave him the business plan. All of a sudden, he started shaking and he forced himself to sit up. He grabbed me around the shirt collar and said, "Don't let those bloodsuckers near your company!"

Like others, he had the attitude that the venture capital community was composed of "vulture" capitalists. Some of this attitude still exists, and I think in certain cases it is rightfully so. While some people have had bad experiences with venture capitalists, many have had good ones. Part of the problem stems from the fact that people do not know who venture capitalists really are or what they do.

I am not going to cry on your shoulder because times are too damn good, just too good, for venture capitalists right now. There is more money coming into the industry than before. This is due to

131

the successful lobbying effort for reduction of the capital gains tax. It is also due to the removal of impediments to pension funds investing in venture capital pools. As a result, in the last year pension funds have dumped more money into the venture capital community than existed in the prior two decades.

The firm with which I have most recently been connected, Brentwood Associates, is going through good times as well. We are not laughing all the way to the bank, but we are feeling pretty comfortable – Apple Computer, Network Systems, System Industries, Midway Airlines, and, most recently, Fortune Systems, which was a $3 million investment in 1979 that became worth $69 million a month ago.

I would like to talk about the basic concepts that drive most venture capitalists, discuss what makes for a good deal and then let you know the problems that we face. I would also like to talk about the future; but when I do, please remember that I am the guy who told Nolan Bushnell that Pizza Time Theatre was a dumb idea. Now, I apologize to Chuck E. Cheese for the personal insult, and I apologize to my limited partners for the 2,000 percent return they did not get.

So what is venture capital? It is a lot of things. It is the money someone advances you to buy an interview suit. It is the money you borrow on Saturday night for the big date. It is the money someone loaned you or gave you to do anything. But that is not professional venture capital. Professional venture capital is different, and it has been around for a long time.

Queen Isabella is a perfect example of a professional venture capitalist at his or her best. Some crazy entrepreneur showed up and talked to her about another dumb idea. Columbus did not invent the concept that the earth was round. He was working on the "D" part instead of the "R" part. She listened and then asked a lot of people whether they thought it made sense. She called in navigators, the pope, and others and then flew right in the face of their advice. She hocked the family jewels and proceeded to give funding. If she had stopped there, it would have been the same kind of investing as giving somebody money on Saturday night. But she went further. She gave management assistance by suggesting three ships instead of two, and she used her not-so-insignificant influence in recruiting. The queen also did something else that was quite important and that most people do not think that venture capitalists do: she did not take all the profit. She took a hefty slice because she was taking a risk on a person who was getting ready to sail off the edge of the earth according to all of her best advisers, but she left some for Columbus and his crew. (Of course, the crew also got to survive.)

This is essentially the way that modern, effective, institutional venture capitalists work. There are five guidelines that are vital in a venture capitalist's approach to an investment. (These were developed by General Georges Doriot who took over American Research and Development).

1.  Don't try to run the business. You don't know how to do it as a venture capitalist; the entrepreneur knows best. Entrepreneurs can't understand this point because they believe the venture capitalist will try to run the company.
2.  Treat the portfolio companies, these little companies you have invested in, like your own children. Kick them every now and then if they need it, but be fair.
3.  Be a help. Be there when needed. Be an ear, a sounding board, an alter ego, a crying towel.
4.  (I think this is the key.) Do what is necessary to allow the portfolio company the opportunity to achieve the potential you originally thought you saw was there. In other words, don't pull the plug too soon. For example, General Doriot practiced that. If he had not followed that dictum, Digital Equipment Corporation would have been shut down during its second year of operation. By keeping it going at a bad time and by providing management help with Ken Olson, General Doriot's $87,000 became worth well over $600 million.
5.  Be realistic. Don't get swept away. It is very easy to listen to an entrepreneur and start getting fired up. They are persuasive people. But a venture capitalist can't let himself lose his objectivity.

Given these guidelines for modern venture capitalists, what is the business beyond the conceptual level? It is well and good to talk about a concept, but a person can drown in a conceptual lagoon if he is not careful.

What is it that venture capitalists want? It is very simple. We want a very large capital gain and a sane life-style. And it is not clear to me that they go together. The large capital gain is driven by greed, simple enough. The sane life-style is driven by a desire for quality of life. But how can the two be merged? How can the venture capitalist get involved while letting the entrepreneur be free to do what is necessary to develop the products, processes, and markets that are important? The key is to "do good deals," which is similar to the advice to "buy low, sell high." Both are true enough. The practical problem is to actually do it! In doing deals, one goes through a chronological process: select, structure, monitor, and exit. Select a good deal; structure it so that you get the best possible return that you can; monitor it by giving help when needed and following through; and then get out. Go public or sell it to someone. But get your return and do not be greedy. Chronologically, that is the way it goes. However, in order of importance to the venture capitalist, the activities are:

1. The monitoring process;
2. The selection process;
3. The exit procedure; and
4. The structure of the deal.

The only time the structure of a deal truly matters is when the company heads south — when everybody is scrambling for the exits. Because your partners are suddenly calling on you, the venture capitalist wants to have the structure in a position so that he has preference and can at least escape with something. He will never get out with his pride on one of these deals if it goes under, but he may get out with something. So spending a lot of time talking to the venture capitalists about subordinated debentures or preferred stock warrants is not comparatively important. Structure will become an issue, but it is not critical in solidifying the deal done.

Regarding exit, a venture capitalist would like to know how he is going to get out of a deal — how he is going to turn an investment into a capital gain. Right now the new issue market is going crazy. This is why Fortune Systems became such a big deal so quickly. We were able to go to the public, and everyone seems to have liquidity. There is a certain amount of stability given to a company by a public offering, but the timing must be right.

The monitoring process, which I think is the most important factor in a venture capital firm's success, takes the form of providing help when needed. We do a lot of recruiting for our companies.

The recruiting process for the vice-president of marketing or finance, for example, is a time-consuming process. We can help the entrepreneur because we have lots of contacts. We also get as many as 30 résumés a week from people who are interested in jobs. By keeping these on file and reviewing them, we help our companies. Planning is another important monitoring area. When entrepreneurs need new funding, we get involved in the treasury process. We will do whatever is necessary to help the company continue, but we will not become a full-time employee or part of the management team unless it is absolutely necessary to assist a troubled company.

The selection process is affected primarily by the entrepreneur. What is a good deal? How do we select a good deal? Ten times your money in five years is a good deal. We look for that. It is easy to look at one that made it and say, "That was a good deal." But how do you find one? How do you predict what is going to happen?

Most venture capitalists and venture capital firms in the United States have a selection process that has extremely rigid guidelines, with an extraordinarily liberal exception policy! For instance, Brentwood is a high technology start-up investor that requires a minimum investment in the range of $750,000 to $1 million. So why did we invest in an airline company, Midway Airlines? Why did we buy out JBL Speakers? Our liberal exception policy! The structure that we put on a required deal has more to do with the characteristics of the people in the industry and the company itself than it does with a particular industry. (I personally feel that there are millions of dollars to be made in ventures like Pizza Time Theatre. I am a believer now.)

For most venture capitalists there has to be the possibility of seeing a ten-times return on invested money in five years. We do not have to get it (because we usually do not), but we want to see that it is possible. There is no point in a venture capitalist's investing in a company that requires sales to be three times bigger than the projected market. The project must be within the realm of reality. Consequently, the market must be big. A big market has a lot of room in it; it can be segmented, and usually there is some part of it that somebody has forgotten. The market must also be growing. A growing market is extraordinarily forgiving. You would not believe the problems that were encountered with Apple Computer in its early stages. The company made lots of mistakes, but the market was so forgiving! People were ripping that computer off the loading dock. It was incredible! The market grew so fast that the management was able to make mistakes and still do well. Part of the reason for this was that the company had a proprietary edge. That edge – be it a technology or a marketing strategy, for example – is a great incentive for a venture capitalist.

Good partners are important in making an investment. There has been a lot of discussion about whether the venture capital community and small business enterprises can live with big companies. Yes, they can, as long as the goals, the aims, the desires, the needs, and the wants of all partners are the same. When they diverge, there is a problem. It is like going to bed with an elephant. Everything is great until the elephant decides it is uncomfortable and wants to roll over. Then the arrangement is difficult at best and dangerous at times.

The most critical part of a new venture is good management. It is also the most subjective. We can find out about the projections for markets, the technology, and whether there is a proprietary edge. The challenge is ascertaining whether the management is good or bad. The only way to do that is to get to know the management personnel very well by spending time with them. Entrepreneurs become tired of venture capitalists because we are always there, always asking questions.

A venture capitalist needs to know the entrepreneur. He needs to know his weaknesses, strengths, pitfalls, blind spots, and biases. Only by knowing the entrepreneur can he identify where the potential problems may be. Reference checks is one simple but effective technique. Some 15 reference checks on everybody in the management team is not unusual.

An entrepreneur needs a team. In fact, a team approach to starting a company makes a lot of sense because an entrepreneur cannot do it all. It is not surprising that the Dun & Bradstreet failure record, which tracks bankruptcies in corporations, indicates that over 90 percent of companies fail because of management shortcomings. A successful entrepreneur needs to have other people with him. The team does not need to be complete at the start because an entrepreneur can put the pieces together after the company is funded. Al Duncan, who is vice-president of finance for Commodore, the computer company, told me last week that he thought the most important person in the start-up of an entrepreneurial company is the vice-president of common sense. Unfortunately, too few companies have one.

What are the problems? Why would a venture capitalist cry? First, even in good times, entrepreneurs are strange birds. They are smart, bright, and sometimes realistic. But right now on my desk there are about 20 business plans claiming that within three years the companies will be bigger than General Motors. So entrepreneurs have blind spots.

Second, the technology is changing very rapidly, perhaps too rapidly. Show me an engineer who has been out of the mainstream of a particular technology for six months, and I will show you a person who is two years behind.

Third, the marketplace in most of these start-up companies is dynamic, easy to misjudge, and constantly changing. No one ever fulfills his plan. In fact, we have never seen anybody make his plan except one person in whom we did not invest. I have a rule that when I make an investment, I tell those in the company to cancel the first board of directors meeting and mail me their updated projections — because I know they will have changed.

Fourth, all of us have our limits. Entrepreneurs reach thresholds; companies reach thresholds. The skills that were important when a company began are no longer important as it matures. As a result people have to change or they have to leave. And it is difficult to fire the founder of a company. The difficulty is not walking in and saying, "You are out," but the agonizing reach for that point. If the venture capitalist decides to do it, he is usually late.

With a strong entrepreneur, a good leader, and a good team, all of these threats to my sanity are reduced greatly, and all of the problems associated with my not earning a large capital gain are reduced.

What about the future? The venture capital industry is changing. Superfunds are upon us. Kliner-Perkins is at $150 million, and Welch-Carson is at $100 million. Brentwood Associates recently received commitments on $150 million four days before the offering memorandum was put out. They turned away approximately $40 million. That is more money in one fund than went into the entire venture capital community from 1971 to 1975. It is going to be different out there. But the world of venture capitalists is different from the world of entrepreneurs. Venture capitalists are followers.

We go where the entrepreneurs are. Entrepreneurs will be in the driver's seat, which, of course, is a good thing.

I anticipate a two-tiered structure to the venture capital industry. Big funds will handle the $2.5 million to $3 million investments, while small funds will do the $50,000 to $100,000 to $150,000 investments (and provide a lot of help). This arrangement is good for the industry, good for the country, good for the venture capital community , and good for the entrepreneur. On the other hand, there is a shortage of venture capital people; this will create frustrations because a lot of money will be available, but it will not be dispersed quickly enough.

Venture capitalists will follow the entrepreneur because the entrepreneur, not the venture capitalist, is the key to the whole process. Venture capitalists are an integral part of the entrepreneurial spirit, but they are not the key. With apologies to William Faulkner, the entrepreneur will not simply endure; the entrepreneur will prevail.

## REFERENCES

Bylinsky, G. "DNA Can Build Companies, Too." *Fortune*, June 16, 1980.

Gordon, M. "Tomorrow's Hot Issues: Brentwood Associates Has an Eye for Hi-Tech Winners." *Barrons*, January 3, 1983.

Gumpert, D. E. "Venture Capital Becoming More Widely Available." *Harvard Business Review* 57 (January 1979): 58.

Hoadley, W. E. "The Spirit of Entrepreneurial Capitalism Is Very Much Alive, Despite Recession." *Duns Business Monthly* 120 (December 1982): 43.

Larson, J. A. "Venturing Into Venture Capital." *Business Horizons*, vol. 25, September-October 1982.

Liles, Patrick R. *Sustaining the Venture Capital Firm*. Cambridge, Mass.: Management Analysis Center, Inc., 1977.

Murray, T. J. "Venture Capital: The Game Gets Riskier." *Duns Business Monthly*, vol. 119, April 1982.

Rind, K. W. "Venture Capital in High Tech Acquisitions." *Mergers and Acquisitions*, vol. 17, Fall 1982.

Rubel, Stanley M., and E. G. Novothy, eds. *How to Raise and Invest Venture Capital*. New York: Presidents Publishing House, 1971.

Timmons, J. A., and D. E. Gumpert. "Discard Many Old Rules about Getting Venture Capital." *Harvard Business Review*, vol. 60, January-February 1982.

# PANEL DISCUSSION
## RAYMOND W. SMILOR, MODERATOR

*Raymond Smilor*: Among the issues emerging from these presentations three points seem particularly important. First, stability is essential to emerging firms. That is, there must be some understandable rules of the economic game. Even chaos can be dealt with if one knows it's a fact of life. Only when there is no understanding of what may happen or when the rules keep changing is it impossible to plan.

Second, perhaps the basic idea of entrepreneurship is the recognition of a need. If there is no need, there is no market. Only by first identifying a need and then applying the technology to it can one hope to reap a profit. Excellent examples were given in biotechnology: measuring vital signs, implantology, and medical imaging. One of the great benefits of those who have led scientific and technological developments in this country is that very often they didn't know something was impossible. Because of that, they helped to create new industries. In this context the academic-industrial complex that is emerging in the United States is significant.

Third, there is a symbiotic relationship between the venture capitalist and the entrepreneur. Neither side should be too greedy, and both must recognize a strong element of risk. Making a success of a new venture is a little like the manager of a baseball team whispering to his best batter as he walks to the plate, "Triple to left." It's a great idea, but there are lots of obstacles in the way.

I would like each of our experts to give us an idea from his perspective — in electronics, in bioengineering, and in venture capital — on the one or two technologies that he sees in the short term as hot and in the long term as significant.

*Harry Keirns*: I think we are going to see some tremendous strides forward in storage techniques. The world is becoming automated. The need to store and disseminate information is fast growing. In the long term, I see software and the ability to bring the power of the electronics revolution into everyday life through applications as increasingly important. People who can make those wonderful chips do practical things will be very much in demand.

*Robert Nerem*: I would emphasize two areas. One is the imaging area. We are moving toward instruments that don't invade the body.

Anyone who has a key idea in that area will have a winner. The other is the biotechnology area. In the long term, this has to be a real strong part of our economy.

*Lucien Ruby*: I think that the genetic engineering industry will be the biggest industry the United States, if not the world, has ever seen. In the nearer term, if somebody can solve the input-output problem of computer systems to overcome the problem of people not being keyboard friendly, then I think he has a distinct possibility of creating a billion dollar company real quick.

*Raymond Smilor*: What is the significance of location factors in entrepreneurial ventures?

*Harry Keirns*: Austin has been good for our people. Because they are so heavily committed to their jobs, they are often not home; thus their families should enjoy a high quality of life environment. Being a part of a growing, progressive community makes our people feel good and helps in terms of recruiting.

*Robert Nerem*: In addition to quality of life, access — and preferably direct access — to a major medical center is important in the medical area. But interestingly, if these are two criteria, Austin would be eliminated on the basis of no medical center, and Houston would probably be doubtful on the basis of quality of life. But, in fact, good work is going on in both places now — especially in Houston.

*Lucien Ruby*: The only thing about a location that is important with us is the fact that it happens to be where the company and the entrepreneur are. We have investments in Tonopa, Nevada; Knoxville, Tennessee; Bedford, Massachusetts; and all over California. We feel that if the entrepreneur chooses a location, there is a good business reason for it.

*Raymond Smilor*: There are three different ways for an entrepreneur to take advantage of a technology advance. First, it may be possible to build and sell a product based on the technology. In this case a person needs some kind of specific knowledge as well as substantial capital and equipment. Second, a person can improve on a technology by furthering the research and development. In this case, an entrepreneur needs a technological talent. He or she must have a product, be able to raise money, and then produce and sell it. Third, and perhaps the most promising in the short run, is to adapt the technology to a current market need, which involves recognizing the need and adapting the technology to meet it.

## Chapter 12

# Summing Up

George Kozmetsky

As this volume has demonstrated, entrepreneurial education does not always take place in the classroom. I usually tell students, "God didn't say you had to learn everything sitting in a class." Most of the successful people who participated - academicians, government officials, and businessmen — kept emphasizing that a person needs experience and common sense. They were telling us that, given an information explosion, it is impossible for one person to keep up with everything.

Elspeth Rostow posed the tough question: Where are the robust companies coming from? Where are those who have the courage to enter into competition worldwide and at the same time provide more than just the needs of a marketplace? It became clear that capital venturing must do more than get a five or ten times return on initial investments. It also became evident that none of us can hide any longer behind the claim that we do not understand high tech. The commitment, dedication, and intellectual resources that were pulled together at the conference must contribute to the creation of robust companies. In this way we can help provide meaningful lives for Americans. Each of us must find ways to encourage robust activity in our communities. The entrepreneurial spirit, when harnessed to resources, can be the catalyst for this activity.

As the future entrepreneurs, capital venturers, inventors, scientists, and technologists, students have to bring a new meaning to business activity. They must learn for themselves so that they can, in an extremely short period of five years or less, start putting something back into the system.

We can no longer leave our economic security to happy accidents, luck, or the random spin of statistical probability. Our nation must convert science through a creative process of human intellect into a body of technology that is a national and worldwide resource. Only by applying our intellect and our natural, human, and technological resources to current problems and opportunities can we strengthen our businesses, communities, and our nation.

Entrepreneurship, above all, implies integrity, morality, and dedication. Thus it requires that we work together to provide a better world for those who are here and those yet to come.

# Index

# About the
# RGK Foundation

The RGK Foundation was established in 1966 to provide support for medical and educational research. Major emphasis has been placed on the research of connective tissue diseases, particularly scleroderma. The foundation also supports workshops and conferences at educational institutions through which the role of business in U.S. society is examined. Such conferences have been co-sponsored with the Institute for Constructive Capitalism at the University of Texas at Austin and the Keystone Center for Continuing Education in Keystone, Colorado.

The RGK Foundation Building, which opened in October 1981, has a research library and provides research space for scholars in residence. The building's extensive conference facilities have been used for national and international conferences including the International Conference on Scleroderma and the Symposium on Current American Economic Policy. Conferences at the RGK Foundation are designed not only to enhance information exchange on particular topics but also to maintain an interlinkage among business, academia, community, and government.

# About the Institute for Constructive Capitalism

The Institute for Constructive Capitalism (IC$^2$) at the University of Texas at Austin is an innovative national center for the study of capitalism. The institute originates and analyzes information about democratic capitalism through an integrated program of research. IC$^2$ studies are designed to develop alternatives for private sector action aimed at regional and national goals.

The institute's mission is to subject capitalism to the objective scrutiny of academic research and provide ideas about ways in which the private sector may respond more effectively to help solve society's problems in a time of rapid socioeconomic and cultural change.

Some of the specific areas of research and study concentration include: the management of technology; corporate governance and social responsibility; policy analysis; macroconcentration; new methods of economic analysis; regional and territorial planning; public risk assessment; state of capitalism studies; research on the ownership, control, and management of wealth; and evaluation of the decision processes in a free society as well as the determination of attitudes, concerns, and opinions on key issues.

The institute maintains strong interaction between scholarly developments and real world issues by conducting a variety of conferences. IC$^2$ research is published in a series of monographs, policy papers, technical papers, and research articles.

# List of
# Contributors

*Dr. Gerald Albaum* is Professor of Marketing at the University of Oregon. He was a Visiting Professor of Marketing Administration at the University of Texas at Austin and an RGK Foundation Scholar from January to July 1983. He holds positions in several professional associations. His areas of specialization include marketing, international business, and social science research. He has published numerous books, monographs, and articles.

*Alan Chvotkin* is the Minority Chief Counsel to the U.S. Senate Small Business Committee, a position he has held since January 1981. Prior to that time he was the Majority Legal Counsel to the committee. Mr. Chvotkin has been a professional staff member in the Senate for the past eight years, previously serving on the Senate Budget Committee and the Senate Governmental Affairs Committee.

*R. Miller Hicks* is an entrepreneur and risk venture developer. He is President of R. Miller Hicks & Company, an Austin-based development and consulting firm. He is also President of Advance Communications, a specialized media corporation. Mr. Hicks has been Chairman of the Presidential Advisory Committee on Small Business Affairs and Minority Business Ownership. Mr. Hicks is active in civic and political organizations and often contributes to regional and national business periodicals.

*Harry Keirns* is a data processing company executive and Vice-President of KMW Systems, Inc., based in Austin. Mr. Keirns has a great deal of corporate experience. He has worked as manager of systems development for the B. F. Goodrich Tire Company. He has also served as President of Automated Graphic Technology in Champaign, Illinois, and was Director of software and data processing for Gould, Inc., in Boston. Mr. Keirns is a member of the Association of Computing Machinery and the Data Processing Management Association.

*Dr. George Kozmetsky* is Director of the Institute for Constructive Capitalism of the University of Texas at Austin. He holds the academic rank of Professor in the Management and Computer Sciences departments. He also holds the J. Marion West Chair for Constructive Capitalism. Dr. Kozmetsky served from 1966 to 1982 as Dean of the College and Graduate School of Business at the University of Texas, Austin. He came to the university from Teledyne, Inc., of which he was cofounder and Vice-President. He serves on the boards of several corporations. In 1980 he was appointed to the Southern Regional Education Board.

*Dr. Robert F. Lanzilotti* is Professor of Economics and Dean of the Graduate School of Business and School of Accounting of the University of Florida, Gainesville. He is also a member of the Economic Advisory Board to the U.S. Secretary of Commerce. He has worked as a consultant to various national corporations, banks, and law firms and has given testimony before various committees of the U.S. Senate and House of Representatives. Dr. Lanzilotti is the author of six books and numerous articles. His forthcoming book is *Management under Government Intervention: The View from Mt. Scopus*.

*Robert Moeser* has been General Manager of the Communications Products Division of International Business Machines (IBM) in Austin, Texas, since 1978. Prior to this he was in charge of the General Systems Division of the Austin plant. Mr. Moeser has been with IBM for 22 years, during which time he has held several significant management positions, primarily at IBM's Toronto facility.

*Dr. Robert M. Nerem* is Professor and Chairman of the Department of Mechanical Engineering and Director of the Interdisciplinary Program on Biomedical Engineering at the University of Houston. He holds secondary appointments at Baylor College of Medicine and the University of Texas Health Science Center at San Antonio. He is Secretary-Treasurer of the U.S. National Committee on Biomechanics, a member of the Administrative Council of the International Federation for Medical and Biological Engineering, Secretary of the Alliance for Engineering in Medicine and Biology, and Chairman of the Steering Committee of the Houston Biomedical Engineering Program. Dr. Nerem is Associate Editor of the *ASME Journal of Biomechanical Engineering* and the author of more than 50 refereed journal articles.

*Dr. Robert A. Peterson* is the Sam Barshop Professor of Marketing Administration and a Senior Research Fellow at the Institute for Constructive Capitalism, University of Texas at Austin. A former President of the Southwestern Marketing Association and Vice-President of the American Marketing Association, he is currently on the Board of Governors of the Academy of Marketing Science. Dr. Peterson has written several books and published extensively in such journals as *Management Science*, the *Journal of Marketing Research*, the *Journal of Marketing*, the *Journal of Business*, and the *Journal of Applied Psychology*. He serves on the editorial boards of five journals, including the *Journal of Marketing*, the *Journal of Marketing Research*, and *Social Science Quarterly*.

*Elspeth Rostow* was Dean of the Lyndon B. Johnson School of Public Affairs at the University of Texas until May 1983. She currently holds the academic rank of Professor of Government and of American Studies there. Her principal scholarly interest is the institutional analysis of U.S. government. Dean Rostow has taught at major universities in this country and abroad, including appointments at Barnard College, MIT, Cambridge University, and the University of Zurich. She has also lectured for the Department of State in Europe and for the Foreign Service Institute. Dean Rostow is the author of numerous publications.

*Lucien Ruby* is a principal of Brentwood Associates, a Los Angeles-based venture capital firm specializing in early-stage high technology investments. Prior to joining Brentwood Associates, Mr. Ruby was a consultant to the Strategic Planning Institute of Cambridge, Massachusetts, where he was in charge of the Start-Up Business Project. Through this project, the institute offered strategic planning to venture capital firms. He has engaged in various entrepreneurial activities including founding several small companies. Mr. Ruby is currently preparing to start his own venture capital firm specializing in very young start-up firms in the high technology area.

*Charles M. Skibo* is the Senior Vice-President for Operations at MCI in Washington, D.C. Prior to this Mr. Skibo held the position of Senior Vice-President for Planning and Administration at MCI. Mr. Skibo began his career at the Exxon Corporation and had held a number of executive management positions before moving to MCI nearly four years ago.

*George F. Troy* is President of Control Data Business Advisors, Inc., and has also taken on the additional responsibility of Control Data Venture Support Operations. He previously held the position of Senior Vice-President of corporate marketing for Commercial Credit Company, the Minneapolis-based financial services unit of Control Data Corporation of Minneapolis, Minnesota.

*Dr. John A. Welsh* is the Founding Director of the Caruth Institute of Owner-Managed Business, as part of the Edwin L. Cox School of Business at Southern Methodist University (SMU) in Dallas, Texas. Prior to his association with SMU, Dr. Welsh was Treasurer of Thermo Electron Corporation at its founding. He has also been President of Joseph Kaye & Co., Inc., and founder and President of Flow Laboratories, Inc. He is coauthor, with Jerry F. White, of many books including *The Entrepreneur's Master Planning Guide*. He is also coauthor of an instructional television series titled "That's Business."

# About the Editors

*Raymond W. Smilor* is Assistant Director of the Institute for Constructive Capitalism at the Univerity of Texas at Austin. He is also a member of the management faculty and has taught both graduate and undergraduate courses in management, with an emphasis on the management of technology and business history.

Dr. Smilor has served as a Research Fellow for the National Science Foundation for an international exchange program on computers and management between the United States and the Soviet Union. He has planned regional, national, and international conferences and workshops, and he has served as a consultant for business and government.

Dr. Smilor has written and published in the areas of science and technology transfer and exchange, environmental analysis, and the enterprise system. He has edited three previous books: *Territorial/Regional Planning and Development* and *Economic Growth and Planning: Regional and National Perspectives*, both National Science Foundation Publications; and *Small Business and the Entrepreneurial Spirit*.

He earned his Ph.D. in U.S. History at the University of Texas at Austin, where he focused on business history and science and technology.

*Robert Lawrence Kuhn* is a scientist, strategist, scholar, and author at home in the complementary worlds of academic institutions and business corporations. He is Senior Research Fellow in Creative and Innovative Management at the Institute for Constructive Capitalism at the University of Texas at Austin and an Adjunct Professor of Corporate Strategy in the Department of Management and Organizational Behavior at the Graduate School of Business of New York University. He is also Adjunct Professor of Biotechnology and Public Policy at Hahnemann University in Philadelphia where he works with the president of the university in strategic planning and the formation of new research institutes.

Dr. Kuhn is an active business executive and management consultant specializing in new venture formation, the science-business interface, and intersector interaction among industry, academia, and government. He is Executive Vice-President and a director of Eagle Clothes, a nationally prominent retail consultant/operator in softgoods, which he created in its present form and where he is responsible for strategy and finance; he also works with diverse companies, investment groups, and entrepreneurs, creating novel enterprises, structuring financial transactions, arranging corporate financing, and planning mergers and acquisitions. He is on the boards of several entrepreneurial companies in high technology and biomedicine. Previously, he ran a foundation operating concert series, international research projects, and cultural programs, and national media and publishing operations. He founded *Quest* magazine and *Everest House* books.

Dr. Kuhn lectures at numerous symposia and is published, quoted, and interviewed widely. He is the author of a peer-praised research monograph *Mid-Sized Firms: Success Strategies and Methodology* (Praeger, 1982): the coauthor of *The Firm Bond: Linking Individual Commitment and Corporate Success* (Praeger, mid-1984); the coeditor of *Regulatory Risk: Issues and Problems in Restricting Private Enterprise* (Praeger, late 1984); and the editor of *Commercializing Defense-Related Technology* (Praeger, early 1984).

Dr. Kuhn holds a B.A. in Human Biology from Johns Hopkins University, a Ph.D. in Neurophysiology from the Department of Anatomy and Brain Research Institute of the University of California at Los Angeles, and an M.S. in Management from the Sloan School of Management of the Massachusetts Institute of Technology where he was also a Research Affiliate in the Psychology Department and a Sloan Fellow.